Rosa Nouchette Carey

For Lilias

Vol. III

Rosa Nouchette Carey

For Lilias
Vol. III

ISBN/EAN: 9783337040758

Printed in Europe, USA, Canada, Australia, Japan

Cover: Foto ©ninafisch / pixelio.de

More available books at **www.hansebooks.com**

FOR LILIAS.

A Novel.

BY

ROSA NOUCHETTE CAREY,

AUTHOR OF
'WOOED AND MARRIED,' 'NOT LIKE OTHER GIRLS,'
'NELLIE'S MEMORIES,' ETC.

IN THREE VOLUMES.
VOL. III.

LONDON:
RICHARD BENTLEY AND SON,
Publishers in Ordinary to Her Majesty the Queen.
1885.
[*All Rights Reserved.*]

CONTENTS OF VOL. III.

CHAPTER		PAGE
I.	'A DROPPED STITCH'	1
II.	'THEN WHY NOT CARE FOR ME?'	16
III.	'I SHALL LIVE TO BE A VERY OLD WOMAN'	32
IV.	CROSS LIGHTS AND CROSS PURPOSES	52
V.	'SHALL I BRING HIM TO YOU?'	76
VI.	'WE MUST TAKE WHAT HEAVEN SENDS'	93
VII.	'MARJORY, I AM HERE'	111
VIII.	'LIFE'S FITFUL FEVER O'ER'	132
IX.	'YOU WILL SPEAK OPENLY TO ME?'	151
X.	'FOR LILIAS'	166
XI.	THE LETTER OVERLOOKED	181
XII.	HOPE DEFERRED	201
XIII.	'YOU KNEW ME BETTER!'	222
XIV.	UNEXPECTED TIDINGS	243
XV.	'IT WAS A TERRIBLE MISTAKE!'	257
XVI.	'WILL YOU FORGIVE YOUR MOTHER?'	274
XVII.	CONCLUSION	292

FOR LILIAS.

CHAPTER I.

'A DROPPED STITCH.'

'WHY does he call me his darling? He has done it twice. He never used—not even when I was a child,' she thought. But it was more than this that made Marjory's cheek burn; for Mr. Frere had taken the little hand and raised it to his lips; and the unaccustomed caress, coming from the friend whom she reverenced above all men, had strangely embarrassed her.

Marjory had come to the conclusion that Mr. Frere was very unlike himself that night—he was making her afraid of him. But as she reached the top of the staircase, she forgot him for the moment; for Mrs. Carr was closing her door softly and coming forward to meet her. Marjory would have spoken, but Mrs. Carr laid her hand on her lips.

'Hush!' she whispered, 'she is asleep now; we must not wake her. She has been fretting herself ill. I never saw her like this before, and it quite frightened me. I will come into your room, if I may, and then we can talk a little.'

Marjory followed her silently. Mrs. Carr lighted the candles, and then seated herself on the couch, and signed to the girl to place herself beside her.

'I have been very neglectful of my guests this evening,' she said, smoothing her hair caressingly.

Marjory trembled a little. The touch of her mother's hand always excited, instead of soothing her. Sometimes she dared not come near her, lest her strong agitation should overmaster her. Mrs. Carr, as usual, misconstrued it.

'You are cold,' she said kindly; 'will you have your fire lighted? Emma thought it would be too warm for you this evening, but perhaps she was wrong.'

'Oh no, I am warm—quite warm,' returned Marjory hurriedly. 'Please tell me about Lilias. I have been so anxious all the evening. I cannot think what has taken place between her and Mr. Wentworth.'

'My dear,' she returned, with some emotion, 'I am afraid Lilias has behaved very badly—she has refused to marry Hurrell.'

'Refused!—after all her encouragement of him?—impossible! Oh, you must have mistaken her; she could not be so cruel as that!'

'It amounts to a refusal—she will not be engaged to him. After all these months, I may say years, of devotion, she wants to go on as they have been doing. He cannot make her listen to reason.'

'You must talk to her—you must indeed!' exclaimed Marjory earnestly. 'Mr. Frere has been giving Mr. Wentworth his advice.'

'Do you know what he has told him?' very anxiously.

'He has advised him to be very firm. I know he thinks Lilias has been naughty, and deserves to be punished. He wants Mr. Wentworth to assert himself, and not give in to her.'

'Mr. Frere is quite right; he is clear-sighted

and sensible. If Hurrell will only take his advice, there may be some chance for their future happiness. He spoils her dreadfully—he has spoiled her all these years, and she will not believe that his anger will ever last more than four-and-twenty hours. He always makes it up the next day, and so she expects him to-morrow.'

'Do you mean that they have had these scenes before?' asked Marjory, rather aghast at this.

'Once or twice; but from what I can gather, Hurrell has never been quite so angry before. He has frightened her—I can see that plainly. She keeps saying that he will come to-morrow, and ask her pardon for all the hard things he has said; but I hardly think she believes that he will, she looks at me so piteously and asks what I think.'

'If he takes Mr. Frere's advice, he will not come.'

'Then my poor darling will suffer. Marjory, she does love him—she loves him dearly. She is tormenting herself as well as him. She would be engaged to him to-morrow, and happily, if he would not press her to marry for a year or two; but Hurrell will not consent to this.'

'Why not?' in a little surprise. 'If he cares for her so much, a long engagement would not matter.'

'My dear, we are women—we do not know how men feel about these things. Hurrell told her that he considered they had been as good as engaged the last two years, and she could not deny the fact. He has cared for her ever since she was sixteen. She is his one thought—she is everything to him; she has encouraged him; she has accepted all his attentions; there has been a tacit understanding between them all this time; and though I am Lilias's mother, I must say Hurrell has been hardly used.'

'I think so too.'

'There can be no doubt of that; and I am not surprised that his patience is exhausted, and that he has at last risen up against such tyranny. What is play to a girl, is death to a man. She will not tell me all he said. He must have uttered some very bitter things; but he absolutely refused to enter into any indefinite engagement; there must be a specific arrangement on her part that their marriage should not be postponed beyond a few months. Lilias would not agree to this; and you know the rest. Hurrell was too angry to open his mouth to her again, and my poor child has nearly broken her heart over it.'

'The remedy lies in her own hands,' returned Marjory a little coldly.

'Yes, indeed; one word would recall Hurrell to his allegiance. But there was a look upon his face to-night that ought to have warned her. Soft-hearted as he is, I am afraid his pride is too deeply wounded to be healed by any show of penitence on her part, unless she submits to his conditions.'

'If he only keep firmly to them,' murmured Marjory, who was rather dubious on this point.

Mrs. Carr sighed.

'Lilias is making herself quite ill over it. Marjory, have you ever heard her complain of palpitations before? Do you know, I was quite frightened; her lips were blue, and I was obliged to give her sal-volatile. I had to use all my authority to induce her to leave off talking, and be quiet. She is sleeping with me to-night; I feel so anxious about her, that I could not trust her out of my sight.'

'Mr. Frere thinks she has more spirit than strength,' was Marjory's cautious reply.

'My children take after their father,' returned Mrs. Carr mournfully. 'Philip was very delicate —none of the Carrs were strong: they all died in their prime. Sometimes I am afraid Lilias has not a robust constitution. I have watched her when she has been asleep, and it has grieved me to see how fragile she looks; but in the daytime my fears leave me—she is so merry, so full of life, so different to my poor boy Barry.'

'But he is better,' interrupted Marjory soothingly. 'You said yourself, yesterday, that he suffered far less than he did at Whitecliffe.'

'Yes, yes; I must not be too anxious,' she returned; but there were tears in the beautiful grey eyes. 'But I have only those two, and I was left a widow early. Now, my dear, I have burthened you enough with our troubles; but you are so affectionate and sympathetic, that I forget you are not one of us.'

'I could not love you more,' began Marjory, in an agitated tone; and then she stopped, and turned very pale. What was she saying?

'I know you are fond of us,' returned Mrs. Carr kindly, and she put her arms round the girl and kissed her. 'Good-night, my dear; I am ashamed of having kept you up so long.' But Marjory did not respond to her kisses; only, when she left the room, the poor girl hid her face on her arms, and cried long and bitterly.

'"I forget you are not one of us." Oh, mother—mother! how could you say that to me?'

When Marjory woke the next morning, the rain was beating against the window-panes. She lay and listened to it as though it were music; and her first thoughts were, that Mr. Frere could not ask her to walk with him, and that she would be safe from his questions this one day. But if it had been bright sunshine, Mr. Frere could not have looked more cheerful, as he stood on the rug reading his paper. Mrs. Carr was already at the breakfast-table, but Lilias's place was empty.

Marjory asked after her in a whisper.

'She is better. She will be down presently,' answered Mrs. Carr. 'You must not take any notice if she is rather out of spirits this morning. Mr. Frere, are you ready for your coffee—and shall Marjory give you a cutlet?'

Mr. Frere laid down his paper, and was alert

and full of talk in a moment. If his hostess looked a little grave and worn, and Marjory had dark lines under her eyes as though she had not slept well, he took no notice of either fact. There was an article on model lodging-houses for artisans in the paper, which he told Marjory would please Anne immensely, and he took a great deal of pains to explain the whole plan and design to them both in his usual eloquent way. Then he strayed a little to the subject of poor-laws, which rather perplexed the two women; and, after that, he wound up with a dissertation on the phonetic structure of language, and the immense difficulty of producing a Cumbrian glossary, to which they lent a very imperfect attention.

'You may observe,' he began, 'that in the phonetic structure of a language there is an immense disadvantage and difficulty. The varying powers of English characters, for example, would produce abundant confusion, and the vocalism of the Cumbrian dialects gives us striking phenomena.'

'Oh dear!' observed Marjory below her breath, and a straggling little sunbeam of a smile came to her lips.

Perhaps this was what Mr. Frere wanted, for he went on still more cheerfully:

'During the European transit of the Hiberno-Celts and Scandinavians, some great changes of the labial organs took place. For example, the Irish and Scandinavian languages lost the initial *P*.'

'Mrs. Carr,' exclaimed Marjory in desperation, and now all her dimples were in full play, 'may I fetch my embroidery? I shall be able to get on nicely with it this wet morning, unless Barry wants me to read to him.'

And though this was dreadfully rude on Marjory's part, Mr. Frere did not in the least resent it. He only took up his paper again, and his eyes twinkled a little behind it.

Barry was occupied with his tutor, so Marjory had full liberty for the morning. She and Mrs. Carr worked a little silently until Lilias joined them, and then they both made an effort to be extremely cheerful.

Lilias looked pale, and seemed somewhat depressed. She had letters to write, and when they were finished she took up a book and placed herself by the fire as though she were chilly.

But every now and then Marjory noticed that

she looked out anxiously at the falling rain, and her mouth took sorrowful curves like a child's. 'She is afraid the rain will keep him away,' thought Marjory.

After luncheon the clouds showed signs of breaking, and Mr. Frere announced his intention of putting on his mackintosh and walking over to Thorpe.

Lilias started, and a faint colour came into her cheeks. He had not asked either her or Marjory to accompany him.

'It was far too wet for any but amphibious animals,' he said; but as he went to the door to reconnoitre the prospect, she followed him.

'You are going to Thorpe,' she said timidly. 'Would you mind giving this little parcel to Mrs. Wentworth? It is the pattern she wanted for a couvre-pied. I meant to have taken it to-day.'

'The rain will be a capital excuse,' he answered cheerfully.

'Oh yes; it is far too wet,' she repeated rather absently. 'I hope you will stay and talk to her a little—she will be so dull. And if you see Mr. Wentworth——'

But here she faltered, and her cheek became very pink indeed.

'Of course I shall see the squire,' he returned, averting his eyes, for her confusion was very great. 'I can give him any message you like to send.'

'Oh, I have no message,' she returned rather piteously; 'only I shall be glad if he would let us know how poor Meybrick is. Mother and I think we shall be able to help him a little, if he will only let us know more about the case.'

'And is that all?' he asked, looking at her kindly.

'Oh, I have no message—no message at all,' she returned hurriedly; 'only that about poor Meybrick.'

But as Mr. Frere went down the flooded path, he told himself that no message could have been plainer—it was bidding him come and give her a full account of his *protégé*.

'Poor little girl!' he said rather pityingly, for the innocent sorrow in her eyes had touched him in spite of himself; but all the same he knew that she would look for the young squire in vain.

It was a long, dreary afternoon, in spite of all Marjory's efforts to entertain her friends.

She read aloud to them ; she talked to Barry ; she poured out the tea, because Lilias complained that her head ached ; and she made cheerful remarks on the weather every now and then. The rain had quite stopped, she said; there was a gleam of sunshine behind the castle ; she was sure they would have a fine day on the morrow ; Lilias must drive Mr. Frere over to St. Theobald's, and show him the church, for he was very learned about ecclesiastical architecture—he had written an article on the restoration of churches once, that had excited a great deal of attention—and he would be so pleased with St. Theobald's.

She was still talking about Mr. Frere, when his footsteps were heard on the gravel underneath the window, and she hastened to admit him : for it was the quaint and friendly custom at Mavisbank for any of the family to open the outer door, and admit the guest into Cosy Nook ; and it was rare indeed for Fleming to make his appearance when they were gathered in the hall. It was one of Mrs. Carr's large notions of hospitality and service, which were often opposed to mere conventionality.

Marjory received a pleasant smile, and then

he came forward into the firelight. He was alone, and a shade had fallen on Lilias's face.

He did not speak to her. Perhaps, with his usual tact, he was waiting for her to recover from her disappointment. He had messages to deliver from the châtelaine of Redlands, as he called her, both to Mrs. Carr and Marjory; and he had a great deal to say about the wetness of the roads, and the effect of the rain-clouds on the hills; and then, by-and-by, he addressed Lilias quite casually.

'Mr. Wentworth will write about the Meybricks to your mother,' he said, apparently apostrophizing the fire. 'He is very busy just now—extremely busy; one of his farms has changed hands, and there are repairs wanted. If he does not come for a day or two, you must not be surprised.'

'Hurrell is a good business man,' interrupted Mrs. Carr hurriedly. 'Of course we must not expect him if he be busy.'

She spoke quickly, to shield her daughter.

Lilias's lip was quivering, and there was a misty look in her eyes. Hurrell too busy to come to her when she wanted him so!—to write to her mother and not to her!—oh, then he must be angry with her indeed!

'Lilias, darling, I wish you would put my knitting straight for me; I have dropped a stitch somewhere.'

And as Lilias rose silently, and knelt down by Mrs. Carr's chair to rectify the work, her face was in shadow, and no one noticed that the tears were falling one by one on the fleecy wool.

'A dropped stitch!' observed Mr. Frere, in a musing tone. 'What a moral is conveyed in those two words! One little mistake—a single stitch lost—and the whole work is unravelled, marred, and out of harmony. I hope you will pick it up, Miss Carr; there is not often time to be lost in remedying this sort of mistake. My sister taught me this; women are philosophers sometimes. Don't you remember, Marjory, how Anne used to say that of all things she dreaded a dropped stitch?'

CHAPTER II.

'THEN WHY NOT CARE FOR ME?'

MARJORY'S prognostication of the weather was correct. When she woke the next morning, the sunshine lay on the dewy lawn, and the birds were singing in the Mavis Woods as though clouds and rain and sorrowful hearts were unknown in their little world.

It reminded Marjory of her first morning, when she went up the dark paths, and found the squire in his woodman's dress, working in the little dell. 'If this be vanity,' she could hear him singing. Poor Mr. Wentworth! she thought; he would be scarcely in the mood to sing that song now.

A pang of sincere pity crossed her when she came downstairs, and saw Lilias's pale face and tired eyes. But Lilias was not to be pitied. She was talking as fast as ever to Mr. Frere, and laughing at him in her old way. And she would not be quiet—no, not for a moment. But if a dog barked, or there was the least sound outside, she started nervously, and her hands trembled.

'Marjory,' she said presently, when she had finished some absurd argument with Mr. Frere, 'I have promised to drive your friend to St. Theobald's this afternoon; but you must amuse him this morning, for I am going over to the Vicarage and to the schools, and perhaps I may call upon Margaret; and my hands are so full of business that I shall have no time at all before luncheon.'

'What a very Irish speech, Miss Carr!'

'I mean,' she said, reddening a little, 'that I shall have no time to amuse any idle people. I shall leave you and Marjory to your own devices.'

'They will be tolerably harmless,' he answered carelessly. 'What do you say, Marjory—shall we make hay while the sun shines? I have not seen the Mavis Woods yet. Do you think they will be too wet for you—or will you show me one of your favourite walks?'

'We might try the woods,' she answered, with a very doubtful face. 'If we find the paths under water, we can make our way down the hill towards Thorpe.'

'Thorpe? Oh, it is always Thorpe!' observed Lilias, rather pettishly. 'Mr. Frere was there yesterday and the day before. He will think there is no other place worth seeing.'

'Do you know, I have taken a fancy to it,' he answered, apparently in good faith. 'It is quite a story-book village. One could weave a whole romance out of that old house—Redlands—and that pretty church and vicarage. I really think one could live out one's life there very happily. There is an atmosphere of peace about the whole place. I like the trout stream—or the beck, as you call it—and the little bridge, and the ducks and the geese, and the brown-faced babies on the green. I said so to the squire yesterday, and——'

'You are very good at description,' interrupted Lilias, with a little laugh; but there was not an atom of colour in her face. 'Thorpe is a very ordinary village. I could show you others that are far prettier, and ducks and geese and babies by the dozen. It is not Arcadia—far from it.

There are spiteful people, and stupid gossip, and humdrum lives even in Thorpe.' And when she had finished this malicious speech, she asked her mother, a little irritably, why they were sitting so long, when breakfast had been over half an hour ago; and this, of course, dispersed the party.

'Do not keep me waiting, Marjory,' observed Mr. Frere quietly, as he took his paper and seated himself on the circular seat in the window that looked over the Mavis Woods, and Marjory had no excuse for lingering. She only stopped a moment to put her arm round Lilias as she passed her.

'Sissie dear,' she whispered—for she sometimes called her by this name since their talk—'are you sure that you do not want me? Mr. Frere is quite accustomed to walk alone.'

'No; I am too busy to need a companion to-day,' returned Lilias, rather impatiently. 'One must be alone sometimes; and you do not pay Mr. Frere sufficient attention. You are unkind to him, Marjory, and he is so good. I never knew anyone so good.'

And Marjory was so astonished at this unexpected home-thrust, that she actually made no answer. She had no idea that Lilias's speech had been overheard in the distant window-seat.

When she joined Mr. Frere a few minutes later, she found him pacing up and down the lawn. He came at once to her side.

'You look very well this morning,' he said approvingly. 'I mean that soft, fawn-coloured gown just suits you. I like your taste, Marjory. All your gowns seem to belong to you somehow. Other people strike me as though they tried to fit themselves to their clothes.'

This little compliment pleased her. She had put on her new gown to do him honour. She told him so frankly, and then she would have changed the subject.

'Poor dear Lilias!' she began; 'it is easy to see how restless and miserable she feels this morning——' but to her surprise he checked her at once.

'Never mind about that; things must take their course there, and it is not our part to play Providence. We have not come out to talk about your friend Lilias; there is a subject nearer home that interests me more.'

'You mean about Anne,' she answered, drawing her breath a little hard, but fencing with him. 'Well, I am disappointed that she has not written this morning; but I dare say we shall hear from her to-morrow.'

'No doubt; but Anne was not in my thoughts when I spoke. Marjory, has the time come for you to tell me your trouble?'

Ever since he had arrived she had dreaded some such question as this. He was not to be hoodwinked, she knew that well; no assertion on her part that she was happy, quite happy, would blind him to the existence of some secret trouble. Truth, and nothing but the truth, would satisfy him; but her lips were sealed now as then.

'Yes, I will tell you'—was not that what she had said when he had pleaded with her so earnestly and yet so tenderly for her confidence? 'I will tell you, but not now. When the time comes for me to speak, you will not need to ask me. I will come to you of my own accord.' Had he forgotten her words already, when she had wept before him and wished herself again a little child?

She pressed her lips together, and made him no answer.

'Has the time come yet, Marjory?' he repeated in the same quiet tones.

'No,' she returned, standing still in the narrow path as though she were driven to bay, 'it has not come; I do not know when it will. I know nothing, except that I will keep my promise to you; one day I will tell you all—but not now! No, no!' with a sudden shiver; 'not one word—not one single word.'

'Let us walk on,' he said abruptly. You have nothing to tell me. Well, so be it; but there is much, very much, that I must say. You will not deceive me long, Marjory,' he continued. 'I shall find out your trouble; you cannot keep it hidden from me much longer. When I set myself to do a thing I generally achieve my purpose. My will is set on this.'

'Oh no!' she cried, in sudden terror; 'you will not be so ungenerous. It is not your trouble—it is mine. I have a right to keep it to myself if I wish to do so.'

'I cannot permit you that right,' he answered, and there was a stern inflection in his voice. 'Listen to me, Marjory. You are young, very young. You have no knowledge, no experience of the world. You are not able to judge for yourself in this. My dear, I see so sad a change in you; and yet you are not ill? When you look at me with one of your old smiles, you are the same Marjory; but when you are silent—when you sit at your work, and you think no one is noticing you—it is another Marjory I see.'

'You have no right to watch me so,' she returned angrily. 'No right—no right at all!'

'Have I not?' he answered, with a singular smile. 'I think I have the right, Marjory, for there is no one in the world who loves you in the same way as I do—no one who feels for you as I feel, my darling.'

They had reached the dell; and as he spoke they were standing before the bench with the carved words 'For Lilias' before their eyes.

Marjory repeated them absently, and then she said, without looking up, 'I did not mean to be unkind, but you press me too much. I know you care for me; you have always been too good to me.'

'My dear,' he returned very gently, but she heard the trembling in his voice, 'will you sit down here?' But he did not take his place beside her. He took off his felt hat as though he were suddenly oppressed, and the arrowy sunbeams fell aslant on his silvery-grey hair, and on the brown keen face; but his eyes were lowered, and she could not see their expression.

'Will you not rest too?' she asked him a little timidly.

'No!' he said, in a quick strange voice; 'I cannot rest; there will be no rest in the world for me, unless it is in my power to make you love me as I love you.'

'What do you mean?' she asked in a frightened tone, for the sad pleading of his voice smote her with a dull pain. 'Mr. Frere,' touching him with her little ungloved hand, 'I have been naughty, I know; but I have always loved you—dearly, dearly!'

'Not as I love you,' he answered passionately, and now not even Marjory could mistake the meaning of his words. 'You have grown up under my roof; you are my sister's adopted child. I have seen you grow from a lovely child into a lovelier woman, but I never knew that it would come to this—that my peace of mind, my content, would be lost, unless I could teach you to love me well enough to become my wife.'

He would have taken her hand as he spoke, but she shrank from him and covered her face.

'Oh no!' she sobbed; and he could see the tears trickling through her fingers; 'you must be dreaming—it is not so. You cannot mean that.'

'On my life I mean it! It is the truth, my darling. You are the one—the only woman in the world for me. Marjory, can you give me any hope?—am I too old for you? I know the disparity in our ages. I am a quarter of a century older than you, but I have seen more than one happy marriage even when this has been the case. If I did not think I could make you happy, dear, I would not ask to be your husband.'

She was trembling so that she could hardly answer him, but he understood her to whisper that it was not that she minded.

'Then what is it?' he asked. And as a sudden fear crossed him, 'Good heavens, Marjory, you are not going to tell me that you care for some one else!'

'Oh no!' she stammered; but she would not

look at him. 'I have never cared for anyone—not in that way; I do not believe I ever shall.'

'Then why not care for me?' he said, sitting down beside her, and trying to draw down her hands. He hardly knew if this was girlish embarrassment or whether he had really frightened her. 'Marjory, be frank; be your own true self, and tell me how you feel about this.'

He could see that she was trying to obey him. She checked her tears; and though she still trembled exceedingly, she answered him bravely.

'Mr. Frere,' she said, in a low voice, 'I never knew—how could I?—that you cared for me in that way; it makes me so unhappy. Oh, I have never felt quite so unhappy before. I feel as though I have lost you.'

'Do you mean'—and here his lips turned very white—'that what I have proposed frightens you?'

'Yes, it frightens me,' she returned hurriedly. 'When I said I loved you, I did not mean that. Did you misunderstand me?'

'No, dear; no,' with a heavy sigh. 'I quite understood your innocent speech; but I hoped that, when I showed you what was in my heart——' but she interrupted him.

'Do not hope; do not—do not!'

He was silent, and for a few moments his face was averted. Could he let her see his anguish? and she meant no harm—no harm at all. It was only his unlucky fate; and surely, with his grey hairs, he ought to have known better. He was silent so long that the poor child touched him again in sudden terror, thinking that he was angry with her.

'Well,' he said, turning round, and there was a smile now on his pale face, 'so you and I are to go on as we have been—good friends, and nothing else.'

'If only you are not angry or hurt with me,' she replied, drooping her head a little.

'I am neither,' was his answer. And now he took her hand, and held it firmly; but she never forgot the coldness of the hand that grasped hers, or the sudden pallor of his face, though the old kind smile was there. 'Do not misunderstand me, Marjory. I shall never be either hurt or angry with you. I love you far too well for that.'

'But you will try to care for me a little less,' she half whispered.

'It would be no use for me to try. I could not

leave off loving you; but you shall never be frightened again by me.'

'You took me so by surprise,' she faltered, for she detected a slight bitterness in his voice.

'Yes; I was too abrupt,' he returned gently; 'but it needed a sort of earthquake to show you what I meant. Well, we will talk no more of that. I am an old fool, Marjory; and, of course, I am served right for my folly. What I want to say, my dear, is this: that you need not fear me. I am just the same to you as I always was—your friend, who would give his life to serve you; and the one favour I ask is, that you will never think of this again. Be the old trustful Marjory. Nothing will pain me more than to see you avoid me.'

'I will try,' she answered humbly; and then, in her gratitude and reverence, she raised her young face to his, as though to kiss him. She did it as innocently as though she were a child. But he started back, and the blood suffused his face; and then, with an effort, he commanded himself, and his lips just touched her hair.

'God bless you, dear!' he said gravely. 'Now, will you go back to the house while I indulge in a solitary prowl?' and as she stood a moment hesitating, unwilling to leave him to sad thoughts, he said cheerfully: 'Yes, go, Marjory; it is very damp here. I ought not to have brought you, but it will not hurt a tough old fellow like me;' and then she turned slowly away.

Her heart was very heavy within her. Oh, why could she not love him, when there was no one to compare with him ? Old ! he was not so very old. Could any younger lover have pleaded so well as he ? Her face burnt as she remembered the strange glow in his eyes, the exquisite tenderness of his voice, and his patience with her. It was she who was unworthy of him. Almost she loved him—but not quite—young as she was; Marjory's womanly instincts were not at fault. She did not love him well enough to give him the title of husband, and her heart was sore within her to think of his disappointment and pain. Did Anne know ? she wondered ; and then a little thrill of pardonable triumph came over her to know that she—even she could be loved in that way, and by such a man.

'Oh, if he could only care a little less, or I a little more!' she murmured sorrowfully.

But she would have broken her heart if she could have seen his face as he sat upon the bench in the May sunshine, with his arms folded across his chest, and his mouth stern and rigid with pain.

'There are no fools like old fools!' he muttered. 'I know that well. Could any young fellow suffer as I suffer? What madness, what utter folly, to set my heart on a girl of twenty!—to think that I could find favour in her eyes, when she has known me from a child! And yet such things have happened before; and I believe I could have made her happy. She is peculiar; she is sensitive and dissatisfied. No one will ever understand her as I do; but it will never do to think of this now. I must live down this pain somehow,' he went on, with a groan. 'She must never know or guess how I suffer. Perhaps, if I go away a little while—no, not for a little while; that would be no use. It will be impossible to go back to the old life just yet; she would try to be her frank, sweet self with me—I know she will try, poor child!—but the memory of this talk will be a barrier between us. She could not bear the constraint, neither could I. I must put time and space between us until all this has been forgotten, or until——'

He stopped at that, and his face grew grey with

a mighty pain. 'Well, God bless him, whoever he may be; for he will be Marjory's choice.'

And then he took his stick, and plunged into the thick, leafy woods that lay round him; and he and his sorrow fought out their wrestling-match together, until the spirit of his manhood prevailed, and his old strength returned to him.

CHAPTER III.

'I SHALL LIVE TO BE AN OLD WOMAN.'

MARJORY would have given much if some slight physical discomfort, such as a headache or a sprained ankle, would have given her the excuse for remaining quietly in her room the greater part of the day.

'When would it end?' she wondered, with a sort of angry impatience of her superb health and vitality. 'I suppose, if my heart were breaking, I should still eat and sleep; it is only in novels that the heroine turns night into day, and weeps like Niobe, and goes about the house like a picturesque statue of woe.'

But though Marjory was ready to heap scorn upon herself, she was as unhappy as any girl could be; she was far too warm-hearted and affectionate to be able to inflict pain without suffering herself. Mrs. Carr wondered what ailed her, when she saw her come in. Marjory moved listlessly; her face was almost as pale as Lilias's, and she seemed hardly able to speak.

'What have you done with Mr. Frere, my dear?' she asked quite innocently; but such an overpowering blush crossed the girl's face that she was sorry she had asked the question.

'He—he has gone for a long walk; I was tired, and came back,' stammered Marjory, and she turned her long neck aside, and touched her hair with a quick, embarrassed movement, as though she would shield her burning cheeks from observation.

Mrs. Carr said no more, but she drew her own conclusions. There was a troubled look in Marjory's eyes, a little quiver about the lips, like a child who discovers that it is suddenly unhappy, and cannot understand the feeling: something had evidently gone wrong with her.

'They are all out of sorts—Lilias and Hurrell, and now Marjory, and I am afraid that nice Mr. Frere too,' thought Mrs. Carr, with a sympathetic sigh, and she watched him a little anxiously when he came in just in time to take his place at the luncheon-table.

But here her feminine shrewdness was at fault. Mr. Frere certainly looked very tired, but then he had had a long walk; he was not pale, he was even a little flushed, as though he had hurried and overheated himself. Perhaps he was a trifle graver than usual, but his talk was as fluent as ever. The only thing she could notice was that he gave all his attention to her and Lilias, and that he left Marjory to herself. He and Lilias were planning their afternoon's drive to St. Theobald's; but Marjory, who had been summoning up courage to speak all luncheon-time, suddenly interposed:

'I wish you would take Margaret instead of me,' she said, addressing Lilias; 'she would enjoy the drive so much, and I am tired.'

There was something pleading in her voice, but Lilias was too preoccupied to notice it.

'Oh, what nonsense!' she said, in her quick way. 'You are in an idle mood to-day. You went out with Mr. Frere, and left him to find his way home alone; and now you are pretending to be tired, when you have only to watch me drive Ruby, and admire the scenery.'

'Well, do you know, I think Miss Ainslie would be a most pleasant companion,' observed Mr. Frere, in a leisurely manner. He was not looking at poor Marjory's hot cheeks; and if he was trying to shield her, Lilias certainly did not find it out. 'If Marjory be tired, I propose that we invite Miss Ainslie in her stead. It would be a good move, would it not, if I were to walk down to her house now, and ask her to be ready, and then you can fetch us both.'

'Oh, very well,' returned Lilias nonchalantly; 'if you are going to indulge this lazy child in her whimsies, I have nothing to say against Margaret.' She could have added that it made no difference to her whether Margaret or Marjory went. It was the quick movement, the fresh air and sunshine, for which she craved. She was restless—ill at ease; and any change would be desirable. Care sat beside her wherever she went just now; and not even Ruby's antics and Mr. Frere's arguments would drive that black companion away.

'You will have a dull afternoon, I am afraid, my dear,' observed Mrs. Carr gently, when the others had gone. 'Cardigan wants me to see after some repairs at Haggart's farm, and I shall be obliged to leave you for some hours.'

'Oh, never mind; Barry wants me to read to him,' returned Marjory hastily. And as soon as Barry was settled comfortably on his couch in Cosy Nook, she fetched the book and began at once; but her reading was so mechanical and spiritless that Barry raised himself and peeped over his pillows.

'What is the matter with you?' he asked at last. 'Are you tired, Marjory?'

'Yes—no! Oh, please don't interrupt me,' she answered rather crossly; but her voice was breaking a little, and she would have gone on, only Barry's thin hand was placed on the page.

'How absurd!' he said, in quite an injured voice. 'Do you think I am so selfish that I shall let you amuse me, when you are ready to cry with fatigue? Don't contradict me, Marjory—there are tears in your eyes; you are just dead-beat. Give me the book, and I will read myself to sleep; and just put yourself in that big easy-chair, and I will see that no one disturbs you.'

'Oh, Barry, how good you are to me! I am tired—oh, I am tired to death!' and here a sob trembled in Marjory's throat.

'I will be as good to you as I know how, for you take no end of trouble for me,' returned the boy, with a little laugh. He had heard the sob, but he could not think what had happened to his favourite. 'Shut your eyes, Marjory, and if anyone comes I will say you are asleep; we shall both be the better for a nap.'

Marjory needed no second bidding. The chair he had selected was at the head of the couch; he could not see her if he tried. Marjory's tears could flow now in peace, and no one would be the wiser. Oh, the relief and luxury of those quiet hours! Marjory's head went down upon her hands, and she gave herself up to that bitter-sweet retrospect. How was she to face her old life again? Could Murrell's End be her home and his too, now this wonderful thing had happened? What would Anne say? Would she be angry with her? 'Anne knows none of my troubles; we are in two separate worlds, she and I, just now,' thought Marjory, with that intense craving for sympathy that comes to some natures.

Mrs. Carr thought they were both asleep, they were so still and motionless.

Poor Barry, who had passed a dull afternoon trying to fix his attention on his book, and not to hear certain suspiciously caught breaths behind him, hailed his mother's return with delight; her face had never been more welcome to the poor lad than now.

'Has not Fleming brought the tea? It is past five; and I hoped I should have found Hurrell here. Oh, what will Lilias say when she comes in? I know she expects him, and——'

'Hush, mother! Marjory is there—behind the screen. I think she is asleep.'

'No, I am not asleep. Shall I ring for Fleming, Mrs. Carr?'

Marjory sat up and tossed the hair from her face; and then she came forward in her usual way to free Mrs. Carr from her wraps.

'Thank you, my dear. What have you both been doing? Barry looks hot and restless, and you, you have a headache, Marjory;' but the girl shrank from that clear motherly look, and left the room a little hastily.

'She was tired,' interposed Barry, 'and so I

left her in peace. I was not going to let her bother herself about me, mother. Does not Marjory remind you sometimes of that girl in "Aurora Leigh"?

> ' " Too much hair, perhaps—
> I'll name a fault here for so small a head."
> *   *   *   *   *

I often quote those two lines to myself.'

'You are quite poetical,' laughed his mother; but she understood what he meant at once. Marjory's face often looked over-weighted with its hair, as it did this afternoon. 'It is very uncommon, this look of Marjory's; but you are wrong, Barry: it is not " the small fair face between the darks of hair "—Marjory is not fair at all.'

'No; but the description holds good all the same, mother. Don't you remember how the passage goes on?—

> ' " The low brow—the frank space between the eyes,
> Which always had the brown pathetic look
> Of a dumb creature who had been beaten once,
> And never since was easy with the world."

Marjory never looks quite happy to me. She is so awfully nice and kind. I wish you would do something for her.'

'I would do anything,' returned Mrs. Carr, in a little surprise; but she knew nothing about the smothered sobs that had roused Barry's compassion. Of course, the girl was not happy—one could see that; but then her own child was miserable.

'Oh, Barry, what are we to do if Hurrell does not come soon?' she said, with pardonable egotism.

'Do? Why, nothing at all!' replied her son indignantly, for he was on Hurrell's side, and could not be induced to pity his sister. 'If Lil chooses to treat a fellow shabbily she must bear the brunt of her wrong-doing. I am delighted that Hurrell shows so much spirit;' for in the Mavisbank household there were no secrets, and Barry had been made to understand that things were very wrong indeed.

'Poor darling! she will be so disappointed,' returned Mrs. Carr, with a sigh. And then Marjory came back, and the talk became more general. Marjory made the tea, and waited upon them both very nicely; and she took Barry's teasing in good part when he became mischievous all at once, out of revenge for his silent afternoon.

She only shrank into herself when the wheels of the phaeton were heard outside.

'Are we not late?' observed Lilias, as she stood in the doorway. For one half-minute her eyes scanned the group before her, and then her voice became recklessly gay. 'Oh, Marjory, what you have lost by your laziness! We have had such an afternoon! Margaret and Mr. Frere got on famously together; they were finding out Greek roots or derivations all the way. It was quite amusing to hear them. It gave me an inkling of what the Tower of Babel must be, when unknown tongues were heard for the first time; it frightened Ruby, for she went at such a pace. No, thank you, mother dear; we have had tea at the Vicarage. Mrs. Barton was as kind as possible, and got out her best china in Mr. Frere's honour. They made so much of the gentleman from Moorbridge that his head is quite turned, and he has been laying down the law all the way home.'

'It is a very fine old church, Marjory,' observed Mr. Frere, standing beside her, as he stooped over the fire to warm his hands. 'The highly decorated roof and massive pillars are grand, and so are the arches. Miss Ainslie told me the nave was Early English. She seems well up in ecclesiastical architecture. She is an extremely well-informed person.'

'Oh, it was dreadful to hear them!' rattled on Lilias, with a forced laugh. 'They were about half an hour in the mortuary chapel, talking about the different styles of architecture —the Perpendicular and Wavy, or Decorated periods—and then they went on to archæology, or what they termed the science of antiquities. Think of poor little me, all the time shivering at the hard names with which they pelted each other!'

'Miss Carr, you were an admirable listener. I am sure we never heard your voice all the time we were in the church.'

'Of course not,' she answered wickedly. 'Do you think I would have interrupted your long treatise on the Sedilia. Marjory, I have come to the conclusion that fate has led Mr. Frere to these parts. Nothing but a female Crichton would ever satisfy him. He and Margaret are kindred souls. They both dislike short cuts to knowledge. They are each a walking dictionary, and prefer picking out the longest words for daily use. They are both an abstract of the reasoning power in the highest state of activity.'

'Oh, Lilias, how can you talk such nonsense!' remonstrated Mrs. Carr, a little gravely.

Mr. Frere was still warming his hands, and did not reply; but the hot colour rushed over Marjory's face. She was surprised herself to find how much Lilias's thoughtless speech hurt her. Mr. Frere and Margaret Ainslie kindred souls!—that any woman should claim him!

'Marjory,' he said, in a very low voice, so that no one but herself could hear him, 'I am greatly pleased with this friend of yours. She is a very uncommon person. I have been drawing her out, and I find she has the simplicity of a child, in spite of her great knowledge. If you stay here much longer you will find her a great comfort to you. I am glad, for your sake, that she has taken to you so much.'

The old kind voice and manner—the same thought for her that had guarded her whole life. Could she fail to understand his meaning—that Margaret Ainslie was only a source of interest to him for her sake? Lilias's careless words could not hurt her now.

'Thank you,' she answered, dropping her eyes as she spoke. 'I am glad you like her.'

'What is dear to you must be dear to me,' was his low reply; and he laid his hand lightly, very lightly, on hers for a moment. No one saw the action; but Marjory's heart felt full, almost to bursting, as she quietly followed Lilias from the room. This was how she was forgiven; this was how he comforted her for the pain inflicted on them both. There was no bitterness in his thoughts because she had brought trouble and confusion into his tranquil life. His great love could never wrong her for one single instant.

It was Lilias whose gaiety kept them all alive that evening, for Mr. Frere was very quiet; and Marjory's sudden veil of shyness and gravity was not to be removed. It was Lilias who sang song after song, until her mother refused to hear another note. It was she who set out the chess-table for Mr. Frere and Barry, and hovered about them with light jesting words. It was she who was not tired when they gathered round the fire before separating; tired—she had never felt fresher. And were they all old women, pray, that they should be sent to bed at ten o'clock, when the moon was shining behind the woods, and anyone else would have proposed a stroll?

Mrs. Carr, who noticed Marjory's fagged looks, had to be very firm indeed before Lilias would consent to break up the party.

'You have been dreadfully stupid to-day, Marjory,' she began teasingly, when they stood in the passage a moment. 'You do not speak a word to that nice Mr. Frere; and I am quite in love with him myself, and so is Margaret. You are so grave and proper. You have not laughed once this evening; and it is I who must sing, and talk nonsense, and keep you all up to the mark. Some one must be merry, you know, and that is always my *rôle;* and—oh, Marjory!'

'What is it, dear? Sissie—Lilias—my poor dear—what is it?' and Marjory, in great alarm, threw her arm round the girl, and drew her into the room. Lilias had stopped speaking, and her face was contracted as though with pain; there was a dark look about her mouth, and her face was deadly pale.

'Don't call anyone—it is nothing,' she gasped; but she suffered Marjory to lift her on to the couch, and for a few moments she seemed absolutely past speech. Then a little colour came back into her face, but her hands were cold as ice.

'I have had it before — this pain,' she whispered after a while; 'once at Whitecliffe, the night I was anxious about Barry, and once the evening Hurrell dined here. What can it be? I wonder. I am quite strong; I am never ill—never.'

'Shall I give you a little sal volatile?' asked Marjory, who was kneeling beside her, rubbing her hands. 'There are drops that Mrs. Chard always takes when she has her attacks. I do not know if they would do you good, but sal volatile is always safe. You should speak to Dr. Ainslie, Lilias.'

'So I will. I will speak to him, Marjory, if you will promise not to tell my mother. She was so frightened that night, she never closed her eyes until morning; and we were both awake, though we never spoke. Promise me, Marjory.'

'I will not tell her unless you have another attack,' she returned reluctantly, for she saw it was necessary to soothe Lilias's agitation. 'Now you must drink this, and I will help you to bed;

for you are cold—so dreadfully cold—your teeth are chattering.' And as Lilias offered no remonstrance to this, she soon assisted her to undress.

'There! I am comfortable now,' observed Lilias gratefully, as Marjory placed the pillows under her head. 'You are a good nurse, Marjory; you have a nice firm touch, like mother's. You remind me so of her sometimes; you have beautiful hands like hers, and mine are so ugly.' And Lilias stretched them out on the coverlet, and tried to pout; but Marjory was shocked to see how wan and pinched her face looked.

'Sissie darling,' she said, stroking her fair hair, 'I do think you ought to tell Mrs. Carr how you felt to-night; you should not hide anything from her.'

Lilias shook her head a little impatiently.

'It is nothing—nothing. What a fuss you make about a trifle! Most likely it is indigestion. I have known people have pains and palpitations just from that cause. I will ask Dr. Ainslie to prescribe for me to-morrow.'

'But why not tell Mrs. Carr to-night?' persisted her friend.

'Oh, what an obstinate creature you are!'

returned Lilias fretfully. 'You are as bad as that stupid Miriam, who burst out crying when I told her. The foolish woman made herself quite ill over it; but I remember her drugs were very comforting.'

'You have over-exerted yourself,' replied Marjory very seriously. 'You should not sing and talk quite so much when you do not feel merry. Oh, it is no use pretending,' as Lilias seemed eager to disclaim this; 'when one is anxious or worried, it is best to be quiet and not talk much. Now I will say good-night to you, dear, for I hear Mrs. Carr's step;' and Marjory withdrew to her room with a fresh burthen on her spirits. Were they all wrong about Lilias except Mr. Frere, who thought her so delicate? Never before had Marjory seen such a resemblance between Lilias and Mrs. Chard as she had to-night. Mrs. Chard had heart disease, she knew; but she had some internal complaint as well. Could Lilias have inherited her mother's delicacy, as she, Marjory, had inherited her magnificent constitution and robust health from Mrs. Carr? This was another source of trouble, and kept her in a waking nightmare for hours. She over-slept herself in consequence, and woke late, to find something wet and sweet touching her cheek. It was a little bunch of wood violets and primroses, with the dew still on them. And there was Lilias, rather paler than usual, perhaps, smiling at her sleepy-eyed perplexity.

'You lazy girl!' she said, laughing; 'do you know breakfast is over, and Emma is preparing a tray of good things for you? Mother said she was sure you were not well, and she would not allow you to be roused. And Mr. Frere picked these flowers for you, to bid you good-morning, as he said.'

Marjory's eyes filled at the silent message; but she said hurriedly: 'It is very kind of him; but you—you are better, Lilias?'

'Oh yes,' returned the girl carelessly; 'but I suppose you will grumble and make a fuss if I do not keep my promise and speak to Dr. Ainslie. He will only laugh at me; he always does. Marjory, I have made up my mind that I shall live to be an old—a very old woman, but I am afraid I shall be a very ugly one. You see my nose is rather long, and when my cheeks fall in, it will have rather a nut-cracker effect. Now you will make a lovely old woman.'

'Oh, Lilias!'

But somehow Marjory did not laugh at the girl's drollery; on the contrary, she looked rather wistfully at the sweet face and the soft, smiling mouth. Lilias looked far from well, and there were dark lines under her eyes, but no one else had noticed it.

'Oh, do you know,' observed Lilias suddenly, 'that that tiresome Mr. Frere has had letters this morning that oblige him to go home? Some friend or other—a Colonel Wharton, I think he said—has just arrived from India on sick-leave, and is passing through London; and nothing will do but Mr. Frere must take the mail-train to-night.'

'To-night!' It was Marjory's turn to look pale now.

'Yes, to-night. Of course it is all nonsense, as I tell him; we none of us believe his plausible little story. We are too stupid for him; that is the reason. He finds himself dull, and then you snubbed him or quarrelled with him yesterday—which was it, Marjory? But the result is, he is going off in a huff, though he does look so remarkably pleasant over it all, and does nothing but make us civil little speeches.'

'Oh, Lilias, how you chatter!' exclaimed Marjory, in sudden irritation. 'Do leave me— I want to get up; it is so dreadfully late.' But she was a little ashamed of this outburst when Lilias laughed meaningly in her face. 'You will have plenty of time for a long talk,' she said, in a teasing voice; 'and he has sent you a pretty little message.'

And she went off humming a tune, though the careless notes died away into silence as soon as she was out of hearing.

CHAPTER IV.

CROSS LIGHTS AND CROSS PURPOSES.

MARJORY dressed herself in haste, scarcely giving herself time to do justice to the tempting breakfast that Emma had prepared. But she need not have hurried herself—Cosy Nook was empty when she reached it; and when Mrs. Carr made her appearance, her first words were hardly consolatory.

'Lilias has gone to see Margaret, and Mr. Frere has walked over to Redlands; it is just possible that he may remain there to luncheon. I asked him to bring Hurrell back with him, and he promised to do his best. Anything is better than going on in this way. Lilias is making herself ill, with all her pretended good spirits; it makes me angry with Hurrell when I think of it.'

'Oh no; it is not Mr. Wentworth's fault—you cannot be so unreasonable as that,' answered Marjory, with a faint smile.

'All women are unreasonable, according to your friend's theory. When I see Lilias miserable, I am ready to fight the whole world: that is how a mother feels. Poor Hurrell! no, he is not to blame. His only fault is that he loves her far too well. I think'—with a half-sigh—'that my child was made for a world "where there is neither marrying nor giving in marriage," she is so pure and innocent. There is more of the child than the woman in her nature. Hurrell does not understand this: no man can. He is very good, but Lilias is too vague —too visionary for him. "We are so happy as we are," she says, poor darling! But Hurrell wants his wife—he wants a young mistress in his home: nothing else will content him.'

'You cannot deny that his wishes are reasonable,' returned Marjory gravely.

'Oh no! and he is welcome to my child; but I cannot with my own hands push her out of the nest until her wings are ready for flight. She is trembling on the edge; she cannot make up her mind—that is what it is. Perhaps these three days' absence may do much for Hurrell; but he must come—Mr. Frere must bring him.'

Marjory was silent. She doubted if her friend would approve of this course. Lilias had been punished, but her punishment had been brief; she had only been served with the bread of tears and the water of affliction for three days, though she was making herself ill already. If her lover returned so quickly, would she not triumph too readily, and still persist in her own way?

'Mr. Frere shakes his head, but he promised to do his best to persuade him,' went on Mrs. Carr. 'Oh, I am so sorry, Marjory, that we are losing your friend this evening. He says he must go. He has telegraphed to his club and written to his sister, so he has quite made up his mind. Barry is inconsolable, and indeed we shall all miss him; he is only a new acquaintance, and yet Lilias and I feel as though he were an old friend.'

'I am sorry too,' returned Marjory, in a subdued voice; and then Mrs. Carr was called away to speak to a tenant, and she was left to her own sad thoughts. She had driven him away—well she knew that—and yet how grieved she was to lose him. A sudden yearning came over her to keep him by her—to ask him not to go, for she could not bear to be left with her unhappy thoughts. He must forgive her, and stay; and yet, what if it were better for him to go? She had no experience; she did not know how a man feels in such cases. Might it not be selfish in her to desire this? Perhaps Anne would do him good and comfort him; he would be more at peace at Murrel's End without her.

Marjory was entangling herself in a maze of sorrowful perplexity; the poor girl had never trodden these paths before, and she had nothing to guard her but her own instinctive sense of right —it was a safer guard than she knew. This inward monitor had prompted her refusal yesterday—she did not love Mr. Frere well enough to marry him; and now it bade her let him go, for his own peace of mind.

She had just reached this point, and was feeling very dull and magnanimous, when Lilias returned to coax her to take a stroll.

'Of course it was nonsense,' she remarked lightly; 'Dr. Ainslie sounded me, and just said nothing at all.'

'Nothing at all?'

'Well, next to nothing. He told me not to tire myself, and that I was not to worry about anything, but keep myself cheerful; and he said I had better not go uphill, or run upstairs, if it hurt me. I had sworn him to secrecy, so he could not talk to mother about me; but he made me promise one thing—if I ever felt the same pain again, that I was to send for him, and then, of course, mother and he would put their heads together.'

'Lilias, I do not like this.'

'Oh, what a tiresome thing you are, Marjory! I am sorry now that I said you would make a lovely old woman—you do not deserve such a compliment. Dr. Ainslie was tiresome too: he poked me about, and asked such a lot of questions. And then he pretended I was nervous and excitable—such nonsense! and he would not promise not to tell mother, until I made him understand that if my finger aches, she worries herself to death about it; that if I were dying, I would not have her informed that I was in danger until the last minute—that is what I told him. Why, she would break her heart beforehand, and then there would be no one to nurse me but that fidgety dear old Mrs. Wentworth.' And here the tears came into the lovely hazel eyes. 'I should wish mother to do everything for me.'

'And yet you are to live to be a very old woman!'

'Yes, of course; I told Dr. Ainslie so, and he patted me on the cheek, just as though I were a child, and said if I were good, and took care of myself, he hoped I should live to be a hundred. Just fancy, Marjory! old Nannie Clarke is only eighty-six, and she has no teeth, and nut-cracker jaws, and her face looks as brown and wrinkled as an old piece of parchment. I hope I shall not look like Nannie.'

'Oh dear, no! you will be a lovely old woman, too,' returned Marjory cheerfully; and she would have changed the subject, for she could not feel quite satisfied about Dr. Ainslie's opinion. He had not laughed at her, that was evident; but Lilias's thoughts would run on in the same groove.

She asked Marjory her opinion about old age. Was it really such a dreary time? Old people suffered less than young people—she was sure of that—but then they enjoyed less; life was diluted to them; material warmth was more to them than mental comfort.

'"When the daughters of music shall be brought low." Well, do you know, Marjory,' she went on, 'when I read that description, I seem to get into a dim world: everything is faint and low—existence seems weak and passionless.'

'I don't think I want to be very old!' sighed Marjory, who felt just now that her burthens were too heavy to carry with comfort. 'I wish I were a Buddhist. I begin to believe in a negative happiness.'

But this was too philosophical for Lilias.

'Oh, that is all nonsense!' she returned with impatience. 'We are Christians, and I am determined to be a very good, pious old woman. Depend upon it, Marjory, old people feel like children; only they are children with a past, and that may make them unhappy sometimes. Little things please them — little jokes, a kind word; even the sunshine and the flowers make them happy. People speak of it as second childhood: well, it is just that they are God's poor, tired old children, who are having a little rest before they go home. Oh, we ought to be so good to the old!—I am sure of that. They are the link between us and the angels; they give a hand to each, as it were—to us and to them; but to some of the poor creatures it is a weary climb home.'

Marjory wondered at Lilias's little monologue, but it somehow touched her. Lilias often speculated over things, and her thoughts were always so fresh and innocent, so untouched by worldliness. Mrs. Carr's words recurred to Marjory—she had spoken them without perceiving their real drift: 'My child was made for a world "where there is neither marrying nor giving in marriage."' What if Lilias were never to attain to that old age on which she dwelt so feelingly?

Lilias's serious talk lasted until they reached home, and then her mood changed.

'Mother,' she said, in her pretty, caressing way, rubbing her cheek against Mrs. Carr's, after the manner of an affectionate kitten, 'Marjory agrees with me that you grow more beautiful every day.'

'My dear, what nonsense!'—with a faint, middle-aged blush, that was becoming enough in its way. 'I am quite sure Marjory was too sensible to say anything so ridiculous.'

'Oh, it is only Lil's blarney,' observed Barry coolly; 'it means nothing at all, except that you are to do something very disagreeable for her in the course of the next twenty-four hours.'

Lilias dropped him a little fluttering curtsey.

'Poor boy!' she said calmly; 'you do not like pretty speeches unless they are addressed to you.'

And then she treated him to an harangue that made them laugh.

She kept them all merry at luncheon, and sent Fleming away, and would wait on them herself; and she hummed a little tune perpetually, as she moved lightly about the room.

Mrs. Carr's eyes followed her continually. 'Does she not look pretty? Is she not the sweetest — the dearest?' her eyes seemed to say to Marjory. And indeed the girl's golden hair seemed to catch the sunbeams as they stole in the room; and there was a knot of primroses and violets in her grey dress, very like the one Mr. Frere had gathered for Marjory.

'Only I picked these myself,' observed Lilias, with a meaning laugh, as she noticed a furtive glance at them from Marjory. And then, without any warning, she came up and kissed her in a way that made Marjory colour and shrink into herself.

It was a lovely afternoon. The fire still blazed in Cosy Nook, but the door stood wide open, and the fresh spring breezes swept through the old hall. The girls brought out their embroidery-frames, and seated themselves in the cushioned recess that looked over the Mavis Woods. By tacit consent, neither of them spoke of going out. Barry's invalid chair was brought round presently, but Mrs. Carr did not offer to accompany him as usual. A slight stir of expectancy seemed in the air. Mrs. Carr brought her work to the window, and joined the girls; but Lilias's fun had died a natural death, and there was very little speech between them.

'Will he come ? Will Mr. Frere bring him ?' Those were the words on everyone's lips, but no one spoke them. Even when, an hour later, there were quick, crisp footsteps on the gravel walk, only Mrs. Carr raised her head in expectation; Marjory's eyes were bent on the lily she was working, and Lilias's face was averted, and one little shell-like ear was as pink as possible.

'You are welcome, gentlemen,' observed Mrs. Carr, with elaborate briskness; 'we have been looking for you all the afternoon. Mr. Frere, you ought not to have played truant on your last day—it was shabby of you. How do you do, Hurrell? and what do you mean by performing the part of absentee all this time?'

'I was busy,' returned the young man curtly, and there was a slight sullenness in his voice. 'I should not have come this afternoon, only Mr. Frere told me you wanted to speak to me about business,' he said. And then he shook hands with them all, touching Lilias's hand very quickly and coldly without looking at her, and sat down by Mrs. Carr.

Mrs. Carr's face fell. Could this be Hurrell who spoke so ungraciously? She looked up at him with kind imploring eyes, but the young squire did not seem to notice her anxious glances.

'It was about business you wanted me,' he said moodily. He looked pale, harassed, irritable. Mrs. Carr understood with much sinking of heart that Mr. Frere's mission had been attended with difficulty. Hurrell had come on no embassage of peace.

'Barry has come back, and is in his room,' observed Lilias suddenly, and her needle flew through the cloth. 'Mother, do you not think you and Hurrell had better retire there to talk over your business? Business is such a bore, except to the parties interested in it,' she continued, with a little laugh that seemed to jar somehow, it was so shrill. 'When tea is ready we can call you; but business is such a bore,' finished the girl, with a falter in her voice, for Hurrell was looking at her with anger in his eyes, and there was a dull glow on his face. What was it to him that the sun shone so that Lilias's fair hair had golden gleams in it; that there were flowers in her gown that he had not picked for her? What was it to him that the loveliest colour had come to her face at the sight of him? He was not to be played with any more.

'Yes, let us go into Barry's room,' he said, drawing himself up to his full height, and squaring his shoulders as though they would throw off an invisible burthen. 'I have bored people sufficiently, I know that—I will never willingly do it again.'

'Oh, my dear boy, how can you say so!' exclaimed the anxious woman. 'Lilias never meant to be rude—it is only her fun.'

'Yes, it is only my fun,' returned Lilias, with an odd gleam in her eyes. 'It is in the nature of business to be dry; that is no one's fault. Go with him, mother. Hurrell is always so dreadfully impatient. We will give you notice when tea is ready. Mr. Frere, come here and tell us what you have been doing. Marjory is as hurt as possible with you, leaving us all on this last day. She would have nothing to say to your flowers, you see. I suppose she has left them to wither on her table upstairs.'

'Oh Lilias!' remonstrated Marjory; and there was a sharp pain in her voice. 'Please do not make Mr. Frere think I am so ungrateful.'

'No one would make me believe that,' he said, sitting down beside her, and taking the work out of her hand. 'My flowers are all right, Marjory—I know that;' but Marjory, who knew that she meant to press them and keep them as her choicest treasure, looked so guilty and conscious that he changed the subject.

'Is that how you are going to listen to my

explanation, Miss Carr?' he asked, addressing the girl as she was about to leave the room.

'I shall be back directly. Marjory can tell me all about it afterwards,' she said, a little incoherently; and in pity for her sudden restlessness he let her go.

'It seems we are to be left to ourselves, Marjory,' he continued cheerfully. 'What a grand old hall this is! It is the very heart and living-place of the house. You cannot think what a pretty picture you all made as we stood in the doorway. Mrs. Carr's velvet gown, and this ruby stuff,'—touching the folds of her dress —' and your friend Lilias's hair that looked like a mesh of sunbeams—it will be a pretty picture to carry with me to-night.'

'Oh! must you go?' she said rather piteously at this.

'Yes, indeed; would you have me miss Wharton—a fellow I have not seen since our old college-days? By-the-bye, Marjory, you must tell me what messages I am to deliver to Anne: most likely I shall see her the day after to-morrow.'

'Tell her that I never wanted her so much in my life—but no, that is nonsense; that will only trouble her. Oh, I have no message—no message at all.'

'My poor little child!' he said very softly, just under his breath; and then he said aloud: 'Perhaps it would not do to let her know that. What am I to say to her about your coming home? You will stop longer with these kind people who love you so, will you not—you are not in a hurry to come home?'

'No,' returned Marjory, and her lip trembled; 'I am not coming home just yet.' But as she said the words the strongest longing came over her to go back with him, an intense craving for Anne's face, and the quiet atmosphere of Murrel's End. Her emotion was not lost on him, and his face brightened a little.

'You may come home if you will, Marjory.'

'Yes, I know,' she responded gratefully; 'but I will not come just yet.'

'Will you promise me one thing—not to be unhappy if you stay here?'

'I do not think I shall be happy anywhere just now,' she returned evasively.

'Oh, you are young, my dear,' he said kindly, 'things will grow brighter for you by-and-by if you will only have patience. Marjory, you must remember your promise to me. I shall hold you to that.'

'What promise?' in a half-frightened tone.

'To tell me your trouble some day—to come to me of your own accord and tell it. I can trust you—you will never break your word.'

She shook her head in mute disclaimer of this; so much, at least, she owed to this dear friend. For one moment, as she sat silently beside him in the sweet evening light, a longing came to her to put down her head on his arm, and ask him to take care of her. 'Never mind my want of love—I will make it up in reverence. I know you will be good to me—it will all come right.' Was that what she would say to him? but would he not put her away from him very gently, and refuse to listen? Reverence—a childish affection—would that ever satisfy his great heart?

'I think this will be our real good-bye,' he said presently; and perhaps he marvelled a little at her silence. 'There will be the others by-and-by, and packing and dinner, and I shall go straight from the table. Wentworth has promised to stay and see me off, but he is very glum and impracticable. Marjory, your friend must mind what she is about; he has broken from his traces, and her little hand will not control him any longer. He seems almost too bitter to speak to her.'

'Lilias provoked him. You heard what she said; she ought not to have sent him away like that. Oh, there is Fleming with tea, and Lilias following. Mr. Frere, you must go and coax them to leave business and come back to Cosy Nook.'

'I will do what I can. Supposing you come too, Marjory?'—holding out his hand; but Marjory held back, and he went alone.

Evidently his arguments were successful, or Barry was bored too; for they all made their appearance presently, and Mrs. Carr sat down with a very tired face, while Mr. Wentworth received his cup of tea from Lilias with the gravity of a judge, and stood beside her as he drank it—making dry, commonplace observations about the weather, his mother's health, and Mr. Frere's journey, which Lilias answered with downcast eyes and a flush on her cheeks.

Mrs. Carr watched them with undisguised anxiety.

'Oh, these men!' she groaned once, as Marjory passed her. 'Could any attitude be more rigid and uncompromising than Hurrell's?' she thought.

He looked taller — older; she had never noticed this dignity in him before. His face looked stern and hard, too; his frank blue eyes were clouded and full of suppressed pain. Now and then he pulled his moustache nervously, but that was his only sign of weakness. If Mrs. Carr felt frightened as she watched him, what must have been Lilias's feelings as he stood there looking gloomily in the fire, uttering a dry remark every now and then? Why, it was as though the seas had rolled between them, dividing her from the real Hurrell!

Once she glanced at him in alarm, but he took no notice of her look.

'Have you told Lilias about the new foal, Hurrell?' asked Mrs. Carr desperately; she must say something to rouse him out of his apathy.

'No; I did not think it would interest her,' he returned, moving away from her side as though some thought stung him. 'One grows afraid of boring people.'

'Oh, Hurrell!' exclaimed the poor girl, turning very pale; and the hands that were busy among the tea-cups trembled.

'How am I to know what interests you?' he returned, almost savagely. But he spoke in a very low voice, and suddenly checked himself. 'I am not myself—I will go!'

'No,' she whispered, calling him back by the very pain in her voice; 'it was I who was rude, but I did not mean it, Hurrell. Please do not go—not like this, I mean. Go and talk to Marjory; she looks dull.'

And Hurrell was so far ashamed of himself that he obeyed her; but when he looked up again, Lilias had left the room. It was some time before she returned. Mr. Frere had gone to look after his packing, and Hurrell and Barry were playing chess. Lilias took no notice of them; she crossed the hall quickly, and sat down by Mrs. Carr, and talked to her in a voice so low that her words failed to reach them. As for Marjory, she moved about restlessly, taking up one book after another, and turning over pages aimlessly, without fixing her attention on a word. Everything was horrid, she thought; the only person who could help them all was going away. How dull it was all at once—how cheerless and solitary!

It was better during dinner. Mr. Frere, as usual, threw himself gallantly into the breach; and Hurrell, who was probably ashamed of his sulkiness, tried to promote the conversation. The gentlemen talked chiefly to each other, or to Mrs. Carr; neither of them addressed Lilias, who was sitting beside Mr. Frere, and scarcely raised her eyes. Mr. Frere judged that it was kinder to leave her to herself; and Marjory, who was sad and preoccupied, was equally silent.

Just at the last moment, when the carriage was coming round, Hurrell came up to Mrs. Carr, who was standing holding Lilias's hand.

'I may as well say good-bye now,' he said, with an attempt at a smile. 'Mr. Frere will be ready in a moment.'

'But you are coming back,' she said, in a little surprise. 'I heard you tell Barry that you were coming back from the station to bring him those papers.'

'Oh, true!' he returned, somewhat embarrassed; 'but I only meant to leave them at the door with Fleming—my mother will be expecting me.'

'Oh, it does not matter,' she replied, with some dignity.

But Lilias, who had involuntarily squeezed her mother's hand, said rather quickly and indifferently:

'Oh, it does not matter to-night; perhaps you will be coming to-morrow, or the next day?'

'Well, no,' he said, evading her look and speaking very nervously; 'I shall be busy to-morrow. There are hundreds of things I must do, for I think of going up to London in a day or two.'

'To London?'—and here her voice shook a little. 'How very strange—you go so seldom to London! But it is the gay time—oh, of course, I know it is the gay time: it is you who never care about such things!'

'One must do as other men, sometimes. I have been too much of an anchorite. I shall not be away long—not many weeks; but if I go the day after to-morrow, I may not have time to look in at Mavisbank. Perhaps you will see my mother sometimes, if it will not trouble you; I should not like her to be dull.'

'Oh yes,' returned Lilias, in a pained voice;

'your mother shall not be dull, if we can help it. I hope you will enjoy your visit—and—and your gaiety.'

And now it was she who gave him her hand without looking at him—perhaps because her eyes were full of tears; but in the dim light he could not see that.

'Marjory!' whispered Mrs. Carr, coming to the hall-door, which stood open on that spring night; and the girl, who was looking out absently at the carriage-lights flickering in the darkness, turned round with a little start. 'Did you hear what Hurrell said about his going away to London?'

'Oh yes,' returned Marjory, with an impatient sigh, 'I heard it all. How stupid he is! How tiresome men are!'

'My dear, I have learned a lesson to-night: it is the easy-tempered, kind-hearted man who can be obstinate and a tyrant. But, Marjory, what I have to say is this: Mrs. Moore has sent for me; I have promised to go down to the Vicarage for an hour or two. Lilias will be alone and unhappy—yes, I know she will be unhappy, though she has said good-bye to him so coldly. Stop with her, Marjory; do not leave her; bear with her if she gets irritable and fretful—she does not mean it.'

'Of course I will stop with her,' returned Marjory hurriedly; for just then Mr. Frere was coming towards them with his travelling-plaid over his arm, and she slipped a little farther into the darkness.

'Well, Mrs. Carr,' he said cheerfully, 'I have said good-bye to your daughter; and now I must tell you that I have tested northern hospitality for myself, and I find it has not been over-praised. One day, I hope, you will allow my sister to return it. It will be a real pleasure to her to welcome you to Murrell's End.'

'Perhaps, some day,' she returned, with a smile; and then, as she saw him peering curiously into the dusky corners of the hall, she said, 'There is Marjory, standing outside in her thin white dress, and no covering on her head. I hope you will scold the foolish child, and send her in directly.'

'I am here,' said Marjory, gliding out from the dark porch, for she had heard this. 'Mr. Frere, I am so sorry you must go; but you will give my love to Anne?'

'Yes, dear. But, now, you must not stand

here another moment. Good-bye, my child—good-bye!' for one moment he drew her close to him, and kissed her forehead; and then, as Mr. Wentworth came towards them, he motioned her gently to go in, and without another word took his place in the carriage.

'Good-bye,' she said again, and all her heart seemed to go out to him.

The keen evening breeze blew her white gown about her feet, and lifted the wavy hair; but she took no heed. The lights wavered and shone behind her; from his dark corner he could see her stand there, until the turn of the road hid her from his sight, and then, 'Good-bye for many a long month to come,' he said to himself, 'for it will be that before I shall dare to see your face again.'

CHAPTER V.

'SHALL I BRING HIM TO YOU?'

FLEMING was escorting his mistress to the Vicarage, and Barry, a little wearied by the sudden bustle and movement, had retired to his own room. So when Marjory had quitted her post in the dark porch, she found Lilias standing disconsolately by the great fireplace; she looked pale and miserable, and as Marjory came up to her, she put out her hand with a wan little smile.

'How cold and cheerless it feels! everyone has left me—even my mother. What can Mrs. Moore want with her at this time of night?' rather fretfully. 'But then, she is always so inconsiderate.'

'Mrs. Carr will be back in an hour or two,' returned Marjory brightly.

She was depressed herself, poor girl! But the dull misery in Lilias's eyes touched her, and threw her own troubles into the background.

'Ah! but it will be too late then,' in a scarcely audible voice.

'Too late for what, Sissie dear?' putting her arm round her as they stood side by side. 'Is there anything I can do to make you feel better? Something is troubling you. If you will tell me what it is, I might find some way of helping you. Things may not be so bad as you think; it all depends on how we look at them,' finished Marjory philosophically.

'Oh, do you think so?' turning to her quickly. 'Marjory, it is not easy for me to explain. I am different from other girls. I have never talked to anyone but my mother about—about Hurrell.'

'But if I know all about it, dear; if there be no need for you to tell me anything?' returned Marjory, with great tact. 'Mr. Wentworth is going to London, and you and he are not parting friends. It is that troubles you, is it not? It is so hard when people misunderstand us, and take umbrage at our words. So much pain may be saved by just a word of explanation.'

'Oh, Marjory, how did you find all this out so cleverly? Did you hear what he said just now?—he must have his gaiety like other young men. He who never cared for anything but just his quiet home and his farms. It is miserable enough when one's friends go away hundreds of miles, and one is left behind. But when they go in anger, when they will not listen to a word of reason—then it is intolerable.'

'Is Mr. Wentworth so angry with you?'

She put the question very gently, but Lilias was in too excited and over-wrought a state to answer calmly.

'Oh,' she said, bursting into tears, 'I have never seen him like this before. He is hard—he is almost cruel; but then he is not himself. How did I know he would take it in this dreadful way? I have often said the same things to him before, and he has been a little sorry and vexed, but the next day he has always made it up with me. Would I have hurt him like this if I had known it? He will not look at me—he will not let me say a word to him.

He puts this distance between us just to punish me and make me miserable. Oh, Marjory, if he goes, and I do not see him again, I think it will half kill me. Some things I can bear, but not this—to let Hurrell go, thinking all these dreadful things of me.'

Lilias had poured all this out between her sobs.

'I think it will kill me,' she finished, almost despairingly.

'Shall I bring him to you, then?' asked Marjory quietly. 'He is coming back with the papers for Barry, is he not? Shall I go to him, and say that there is something you have to say to him, and he must come in for a moment?'

A sudden hope shone in Lilias's eyes.

'Do you think he will come? Marjory, dear Marjory, do you think you could persuade him? If I could only just say to him that he misunderstood me—that I never meant what he thought—that he must not go away believing such hard things of me—I should go to sleep more happily. I should not dread the waking.'

'Then I will certainly bring him,' returned Marjory, with a reassuring smile. 'Cheer up,

Sissie dear, and dry your eyes. I do so hate to see you cry; it makes me feel bad. You are always so bright, so full of life, that one cannot imagine you in trouble.'

'I look dreadfully ugly when I cry,' replied Lilias, trying to laugh. 'I cannot understand anyone falling in love with my long pale face. It seems so ridiculous that anyone can care for me.'

'Now you look more like yourself,' observed Marjory, in an approving tone. 'Do you know, you rather shock me—you seem to take trouble so badly; such a little thing makes you ill. Now I am not like that. I am so strong that nothing seems to hurt me, and yet I know what it is to be dreadfully unhappy.'

'You poor dear!' kissing her. 'But, Marjory, you must not say that; Hurrell's anger is not a little thing to me. I believe there are some things that I could bear. If people died, for example, if I lost them in that way—well, I should mourn for them all my life; but there would not be this intolerable sense of loss.'

'Not if she—not if Mrs. Carr were to die?' in a curiously low tone.

'Oh, my mother!' with a sudden exquisite

pathos in her voice. 'God forbid that I should survive her, Marjory! But if it should be so, if she—my mother—went into that other room, —you know what I mean—I might break my heart with longing for the sight of her dear face, but I should never lose her; she would be mine—my mother still. My dear, death does not separate hearts. I am not so poor a Christian that I should believe that.'

'But if you were to lose her in any other way? If she were to be alive, and yet in some strange way you were to be divided?' and there came a singular look into Marjory's eyes.

'How could I lose her, except by death? You strange girl, what can you mean by putting such a question? One's mother is one's mother still, though oceans were to roll between us.'

'Never mind what I mean,' returned Marjory unsteadily. 'I am supposing things, that is all. Oh, I do not mean death, nor am I talking about earthly distances—what would that matter? as you say. But if you had a rival, Lilias, in your mother's heart; if you should find some change in her; if things were different between you— oh, I cannot explain what I mean—I only want to find out what your Christian faith would do for you then?'

'It would do little, I fear,' she returned slowly. 'You are talking strangely, to-night, Marjory; but I think I see the drift of your meaning. You are hinting at some sort of moral separation—something impossible—that could never happen.'

'But if it did happen, Lilias?'

'My dear,' with a sweet, but very fleeting smile, 'such a thing would not vex me long. I should have no strength for such a sorrow as that. Look what these three days have done; they have made me ill. But with my mother! Oh, I could not live if there should be trouble between her and me. Marjory, how frightened you look! Why, we are talking this nonsense just to pass the time, I believe. Oh, you do not know me, or you would not put such questions. Death! well, that is sad; but we have our friends still close beside us, though we do not see them. But a division of heart, unkindness, any shadow of change between those who love each other—it is this that I could not bear; the weight and misery of it would crush my life out.'

'Do not let us talk any more,' returned Marjory, in a hard voice.

A new pang tormented her—a prevision of evil. Lilias's words rang in her ears, and through her heart, many a day after they were spoken : 'Unkindness, any shadow of change between those who love each other—it is this that I could not bear ; the weight and misery of it would crush my life out.' And she had listened to them—she who knew that one day she would rob Lilias of her mother. Marjory's own heart was beating so that she could hardly breathe. It was almost a relief to her that at that moment she could hear the carriage-wheels sounding in the distance. Lilias had heard them too, for she turned suddenly very pale.

'You must go, or you will be too late,' she said, giving Marjory a little push. And Marjory, without another word, opened the door, and ran out into the darkness.

'Is that you, Mr. Wentworth?' she exclaimed, as a dark figure became visible.

But another instant proved to her that it was only the groom walking up to the house with the papers.

'Take them to the door, I must speak to your

master a moment,' she said quickly, as the man in some surprise touched his hat, and seemed about to address her.

The rain was falling slightly, but Marjory did not heed that. She ran down the gravel walk, with her white gown gleaming in the murky light, and in another moment had startled Mr. Wentworth, who had taken his groom's place, and was holding in his fretting mare.

'Lilias!' he exclaimed, and then stopped in some confusion, for that tall figure could not be hers.

'Oh, I am not Lilias, but it is Lilias who wants you. Please go in a moment, Mr. Wentworth; there is something she wishes to say. There is your man coming back, and it will not hurt the mare to stand a little. Please come, for it is raining, and I cannot wait any longer.'

'I think I had better not,' he returned slowly. 'You are very good, Miss Deane, to take this trouble; but please tell her I had better not come in to-night.'

'I shall tell her no such thing,' replied Marjory, roused by this opposition. 'Mr. Wentworth, Lilias is not well; there is something troubling her. She will not sleep to-night if she be crossed. Come,' as he wavered, evidently debating whether he should yield or not, ' five minutes will not hurt your mare, or give Mrs. Wentworth any great anxiety.'

Her sarcasm acted as a spur; he threw the reins to his servant, and prepared to accompany her. Marjory only waited until he closed the gate behind him, and then she ran in.

'He is coming, Lilias!' she panted, as she passed through the hall; 'but it is raining, and my dress is wet;' and with this excuse she disappeared.

'I told Miss Deane that I had better not come in to-night,' observed Mr. Wentworth a little abruptly, as he came forward into the light. 'I knew your mother was out, and it is nearly nine, and the mare is rather fresh; but she said that you wanted to speak to me.'

'I do want to speak to you,' she said, in a pleading voice. 'Hurrell, you may think what you like, but I could not let you go away all that distance, feeling you were angry with me. When people are angry with me, and say hard things, it makes me ill. I do not seem able to bear it.'

'Have you sent for me to tell me that I have

made you ill? Is that likely to do you or me any good?'

'No,' she returned, flushing at this; 'but we have been friends for so many years, that surely I may ask you to forgive me.'

But the same angry glow came over his face as she said this.

'Things have come to a pretty pass, indeed, when there can be a question of forgiveness between you and me! That I should hear you say such words to me, who have worshipped the very ground you trod upon! Oh, Lilias, how can you!' And the poor fellow averted his face, that she should not see how her words moved him.

'Am I not to be forgiven, then?' she returned a little piteously, for she misunderstood him. 'Hurrell, I never meant to hurt you so! You would not listen to me, or I would have explained my meaning better.'

'I quite understood you,' he replied, leaning his head on his hand as he propped himself against the high carved mantelpiece. 'You cared for me a good deal, but not enough to sacrifice your freedom for me. You objected to my conditions; you threw me over after years of encouragement, and denied me what alone could satisfy me. Well, you have your freedom, Lilias: I withdraw my suit. You may have my forgiveness too, if you will—as certainly as you have my love. Well, does that not content you?' as she gave him a most sorrowful look. 'Will you tell me again that I have made you ill?'

'No; it is myself—my own fault. But, Hurrell, what have I done so wrong, after all? I did not want to be married just yet'—blushing painfully as she spoke: 'I said we were happier as we were. Hush! please let me finish,' as he seemed about to interrupt her with some impatience. 'If I had known how it would hurt you, I would not have tried so hard for my own way. Girls are silly sometimes; they do not know what they want. I cannot change my nature. I am foolish, and like a child, I know; but now I have sent for you to say that I will not cause you pain any longer—you shall not be so changed and unlike yourself through me. Hurrell, indeed things shall be as you wish—your will shall be mine in future.'

'What do you mean?' he asked, fixing on her a keen glance, for he could not credit what he heard. 'You are generally so frank, Lilias; you tell me the whole truth about yourself. I have said so much all these years, surely you owe it to me to speak out plainly now.'

'I cannot speak more plainly,' she replied, casting down her eyes, for her confusion was very great. 'Hurrell, you know best what you have wished so long.'

'I have wished for you to be my wife, Lilias. How many times have I asked you?'

'Well, you shall have your wish by-and-by,' in a trembling voice; but Lilias hid her face completely now.

But this time he understood her. If there were bitter tears shed in that self-surrender—if the sacrifice were greater than even he could guess—he knew nothing of it. How could he realize anything but that the wish of his life was granted? his bird was fluttering still, but he had it safely; and as he took the fair head between his hands, and kissed it gently, he bade God bless her for her generous gift.

'Are you happy?' she asked him by-and-by, and her lovely eyes seemed to look wistfully at him.

'Most truly and entirely happy, my dearest!'

'Oh, I am so glad!' and her voice took a little cooing note of pleasure, like a mother who sees her child unexpectedly gratified. 'That is what I wanted. All these days I have said to myself, "If I can only make up to him for my unkindness; what does anything matter if he will only own himself happy?"'

'You darling!—but surely you share my happiness?' rather jealously.

'A little bit,' in her old mischievous voice. 'But I am not going to gratify your vanity any more; for, after all, you behaved very badly, and gave me a great deal of trouble. Now, Hurrell, as it is long past nine, and the mare is so fresh, and——'

But he would not allow her to finish her sentence.

'Oh, you are not going to dismiss me in that fashion!' he said, in an offhand manner. 'Do you suppose the mare is standing out in that rain? Of course, Anderson had his wits about him—he is a sharp lad—and has taken her back to the stable. I am waiting to see your mother, Lilias.' But at the mention of her mother, Lilias grew suddenly grave. 'Now,' he went on, for he was watching her closely, and could almost read her thoughts, 'I am going to talk to you very seriously, and you must be so good as to listen to me. Do you think that all this will make any difference—that I shall ever come between you two—that you should look sad at the mention of her name? She will have two sons, that is all; and we shall each have two mothers. Oh, I know exactly what to expect,' as she looked up at him with a mute expression of gratitude. 'When I come in tired from my magistrate's work, or from tramping over my farms, and ask for my wife—well, I shall have to go to Mavisbank to find her. And if I take you abroad, say on our wedding-trip—and the south of France or Italy will be just the thing for October—of course, we shall find your mother and Barry waiting for us. And pray what have I said, that there should be tears in your eyes?'

'Because you are so good,' she returned, with quivering lips. 'Because I think there is no one so good as you.' And this answer was perfectly satisfactory to the young man.

Marjory, sitting alone in her own room, thought it was long before the opening of the hall-door signified Mrs. Carr's return; and she thought it longer still before the dog-cart was brought round, and Mr. Wentworth's voice was heard calling out a cheerful good-night. Marjory stood and listened, or paced her room restlessly. They had forgotten her, she thought. It was not for her to remind them of her existence; there was much that those two must have to say to each other. But she would not seek her bed until she knew how things were, and if she were to wish Lilias joy.

Presently, towards midnight, she heard their voices, and went out into the passage. They were coming slowly up the staircase hand-in-hand, and both their faces were pale; only there was a bright, excited look in Lilias's eyes. At the sight of Marjory, she gave a little cry.

'Oh, you poor child!' she said, running up to her; 'you are still dressed at this time of night, and we had forgotten you! How unkind and selfish you must have thought us!'

'No, indeed; only I was too anxious to rest. Is it all right, Lilias?—are you going to sleep happily?'

'It is all as it should be,' returned Mrs. Carr cheerfully; 'Lilias has made it up with Hurrell, and atoned for all her bad conduct. Now, you must congratulate us both, Marjory. Lilias is giving me just the son I wanted. Hurrell will take care of us all, and we shall be as happy as possible.'

It struck Marjory that Mrs. Carr spoke as if she were anxious to cheer Lilias; and certainly the girl drew back, and looked a little grave and shy, as Marjory warmly kissed and congratulated her.

' She is tired. All this has tired and excited her,' went on Mrs. Carr, with a quick, warning glance at Marjory not to say any more on the subject. ' When she has had a good night's sleep she will feel better able to realize things. Come, Lilias, Marjory will excuse our talking any more to-night. Hurrell will be coming early to-morrow, and you must be your old bright self.'

And putting her arm gently round the girl's shoulder, she drew her away.

CHAPTER VI.

'WE MUST TAKE WHAT HEAVEN SENDS.'

BUT it was many days before Lilias was her old bright self again; those who watched her closely—Mrs. Carr and Marjory—knew that there was some strain or oppression on the girl's sensitive spirits. Her nervous and delicate organization made itself clearly visible.

When Mr. Wentworth was present, this condition of things was not so noticeable. Her gentle sprightliness returned, and nothing could be more frank and affectionate than her manner when they were alone together. Her one anxiety seemed to make him completely happy, and she certainly succeeded in this.

Hurrell's years of devotion had reaped their reward; the young man seemed almost amazed at his own happiness. His young *fiancée* was so perfectly sweet and submissive. All her little tyrannies, her girlish airs and attempts to subjugate him, seemed buried in the past. If he expressed a wish, she was always desirous to carry it out. If, in the intoxication of his sudden triumph, he grew a little masterful—as men will, though without meaning it—her meekness never gave him a hint that she was not yet his wife. But, indeed, any girl might have been proud of such a lover. Those who saw them together thought that nothing could be more perfect than Hurrell's behaviour. When others were present, he never obtruded his claims on her attention. Only the quiet look of mutual understanding that passed between them spoke of their deep affection.

When Hurrell was with her, Lilias seemed perfectly content; but in his absence, and especially when she was alone with Marjory, she had fits of gravity—silent moods that were somewhat inexplicable: if roused out of these, she grew captious and fretful. Mrs. Carr more than once hinted that she was sure that Lilias was not as well as usual. She did not sleep with her old soundness, and nothing would induce her to sleep alone. She came regularly into Mrs. Carr's room of a night; sometimes she was wakeful, and would talk far into the night, and there was no silencing her; and at other times she would lie in perfect silence, but Mrs. Carr knew that she was not asleep, for every now and then a quick sigh escaped her.

'If I were you, I should consult Dr. Ainslie about her sleeplessness,' observed Marjory very wisely; but she was almost sorry that she had given this hint, for when Mrs. Carr returned from her colloquy with the doctor, her eyes looked as though she had been weeping.

'Oh, Marjory,' she said, when they were alone together, 'I think I am very unhappy about my children. Dr. Ainslie has quite frightened me about Lilias: we have always thought her so strong. But no; he says it is only her spirits. She has a weak heart; at least, he did not tell me exactly what was the matter. But he said any form of excitement was bad for her. A long engagement—well, he would not hold with that; he thought the sooner she was married the better. He thinks so highly of Hurrell—he is just the husband for her. He is so gentle and quiet that he will calm down her excitability.

Perhaps, if they went abroad and lived quietly—but just now she was not strong. It was not so much what he said, but it was his manner, Marjory. Do you think he is keeping back anything from me?'

Of course, Marjory disclaimed this stoutly. Nevertheless, she had an uneasy consciousness in her own mind that Dr. Ainslie had indulged in some mental reservation—as doctors will. She thought Lilias was certainly not herself; such unequal spirits could hardly belong to a healthy condition of mind and body. But she did her best to quiet Mrs. Carr's fears; and very soon a strange occurrence, or rather a series of occurrences, turned their attention into a different channel—happily for Lilias, who would certainly have resented much watchfulness on their part.

It was Lilias who brought them the news, about a fortnight after her own engagement with the young Squire of Redlands. She had been for a walk with Hurrell and Lassie, and he had left her and Lassie to return through the village alone, as he had to transact some business at a farmhouse. Marjory, who looked up from her work with a welcoming smile, was surprised at the flushed and disturbed look on Lilias's face, as she entered the hall.

'Do you know what news I am bringing you back?' she said, in a tone of strong disgust. 'Mother, how can people behave so? I am quite ashamed of him—a clever man like him, and at his age, too.'

Mrs. Carr seemed somewhat perplexed at this speech.

'You are speaking in riddles, my dear,' she said quietly. 'What clever man do you mean? I know of none in this place except Dr. Ainslie, and I certainly know nothing but good of him; there is Mr. Moore, but surely you are not speaking of the Vicar?'

'Oh no. Of course it is Dr. Ainslie. Mother, you are too good and innocent for this world! You would never dream of such a thing unless they forced you to believe it. Poor Margaret! My heart is bleeding for her—such an indignity to be put on her!'

'Really, Lilias, this is too mysterious,' observed Mrs. Carr, smiling. 'I shall begin to think that Dr. Ainslie is going to be married again.'

'And you will think what is true. And to

Katie Stallard, of all people in the world!' and as Marjory started and exclaimed at this, she went on: 'Yes, you were right, Marjory; you were cleverer at finding her out than either mother or I. Think how preposterous it all is! That little round-faced demure girl to be Margaret's step-mother, and Margaret—whose father is everything to her—who has been his companion from a child!'

'I am very grieved and shocked to hear this,' returned Mrs. Carr, who certainly looked both. And then she added quickly: 'Hush, Lilias! don't seem as though you were telling us. There is Katie herself coming up the garden-walk. Where did you get your news—quick!'

'Katie told me. I met her just now; but she never spoke of following me, the sly little puss!'

But here Mrs. Carr gave her a warning look, for the hall-door stood open, in its usual summer fashion, and already Katie was on the threshold.

She came in quickly, and went up to Mrs. Carr, holding out her little gloved hands, in a humble deprecating way.

'Oh, Lilias,' she said, 'have you told them?

I followed you; I wanted to be the first, but you and Lassie were too quick for me—I could not catch you up. I thought you would be all talking of me, and I wanted to hear what you said. Please don't scold me—please don't be hard upon me—you know I cannot help it.'

'This is very strange news, Katie; I hardly know how to believe it,' observed Mrs. Carr, with a gravity that was certainly not promising.

'Oh, please do not say so!' implored Katie, with a flickering of her light eyelashes. 'How could I help saying "Yes"—a poor lonely little creature as I am—when that good man—he is a good man, is he not, Mrs. Carr?—offered me the shelter of his home?'

'But you have a good home at the Vicarage, Katie, and Mrs. Moore treats you as her own daughter; and, my dear, forgive me if I say what is the truth, Dr. Ainslie is old enough to be your father.'

'Oh, what does that matter?' returned Miss Stallard, clasping her hands; but her pink cheeks deepened a little. 'I never cared for young men—never; they are so vapid and egotistical. It is themselves they think about,

not us; but I have always reverenced grey hair.
What does it matter about the disparity in our
ages, if I can only be a comfort to him?'

'But, Katie, have you considered Margaret's
feelings in this? Remember, she has been
everything to her father ever since her mother
died. I am afraid this will be a great trial to
her——'

But she was interrupted.

'How can you say such things, my dear Mrs.
Carr? I doat on Margaret. Ask Dr. Ainslie
if I have not the very highest opinion of her.
If she be a little visionary and impracticable,
those are not grievous faults; I am sure we
shall be the most united household possible.
You know there is nothing I love so much as
to be useful; housekeeping is a pleasure to me.
Oh, we shall arrange everything admirably;
dear Margaret will be free to doctor the sick
people, and teach in the schools, and be the St.
Kilda's factotum, and I can relieve her from all
domestic drudgery.'

Mrs. Carr made no answer to this. Perhaps
she found it difficult to adjust her thoughts; but
Lilias, who had sat by in indignant silence,
observed in a slightly sarcastic tone:

'I hope Margaret likes this division of duties. Is the wedding to be soon, Katie?'

But at this harmless question, Miss Stallard seemed for the first time really embarrassed.

'Dr. Ainslie wishes it,' she stammered. 'There is to be no fuss, no ceremony; dear Mrs. Moore is not to be troubled. I am to go to church in my travelling-dress. I am afraid you will be shocked, Mrs. Carr; but Dr. Ainslie says, at his age, any waiting would be absurd. Thursday week—that is the day. Of course I must be guided by his wishes.'

'Thursday week!' ejaculated Lilias; and then she said, in rather a cool tone, 'Does Margaret know this?'

'Her father told her last night,' returned Miss Stallard, with an uncomfortable blush. Mrs. Moore only knew yesterday; and of course she was the first to be told. No one is nice to me about it,' went on Katie, looking up appealingly with innocent blue eyes. 'Mrs. Moore cried, and said I was an unfeeling girl to leave her with all those children on her hands. She counted on me to put it off for three months; but I hope that I convinced her that I could do nothing of the kind. "Dr. Ainslie has chosen me—a poor, penniless little governess"—that is what I said to her. "Do you think, after all his goodness and generosity, that I could go against his expressed wishes?" And of course, after that, she could say nothing.'

'I think it is a pity Dr. Ainslie is in such a hurry,' observed Mrs. Carr quietly. 'Mrs. Moore has been like a mother to you, Katie; no one could have been kinder. Would it not have been better if you had put off your marriage until she had found some one to take your place? Poor woman! it is certainly rather hard to have all those children left on her hands!'

'We have thought of that,' replied Miss Stallard quickly. 'Dr. Ainslie and I have talked it over together. He quite agrees with me that it will just suit Margaret—at least for the present. You know she has a perfect passion for teaching—it comes as naturally to her as housekeeping does to me. I was never intended for a governess—never! a stupid little thing like me—but dear Margaret loves it of all things. I talked it over with Dr. Ainslie, and he promised to speak to Margaret about it; and so I dropped a hint to Mrs. Moore. "I am sure dear Margaret will overlook Edith's and Helena's lessons; and perhaps she would not mind teaching Bessie, and Goody, and Goosey for the present.'

'I hope you did not say this without consulting Margaret,' remonstrated Lilias ; but Miss Stallard only laughed at her grave tone.

'My dear Lilias, of course Dr. Ainslie will say what he likes to his own daughter. What have I to do with it ? I shall never come between them—never ! If I drop a hint or an opinion, and he thinks proper to act upon it, that is not my affair. What I said to him was very simple : " Mrs. Moore is dreadfully put out with me ; I wish I could find a substitute for myself. I should be happier in my mind if I could arrange something. Dear Margaret is always full of schemes for joining the Zenana Mission I wish we could persuade her that a home mission would be just as useful. Those dear children, now—well, would not that be a work worthy of our Margaret ?" '

'I think you stated your wishes very plainly.'

'I—I have no wishes,' and here the sandy eyelashes twitched a little nervously. 'I always say frankly what I think ; that is the best plan, is it not? Dr. Ainslie is so good and considerate, he wanted me to have my mother and one or two of my sisters up for our wedding. But I said no; dear Mrs. Moore must not be troubled. No one shall be burthened with my relations. If he chose to marry a poor girl, his generosity should not be abused. Goody and Goosey shall put on their clean white frocks and be my bridesmaids, but there shall be no fuss, no ceremony at all; and Dr. Ainslie quite approves of it all.'

'Well, I wish you every happiness, Katie,' observed Mrs. Carr, but her tone was without enthusiasm. She kissed the girl rather coldly, as she took her leave. 'Lilias,' she said, shaking her head, when their visitor had departed, 'I am not pleased about this. Poor Margaret will be dreadfully cut up! She will feel as though she has lost her father. I think you and Marjory had better go down to her after luncheon, and I will go across to the Vicarage and condole with Mrs. Moore. I feel very angry with Dr. Ainslie, at his age, to marry a girl like Katie. I am disappointed in her, too. I do not like the way she speaks about Margaret; it is too patronizing—it is not nice in one so much younger. Oh, my dears, what a world this is!' and Mrs. Carr sighed as she laid aside her embroidery.

Marjory's opinion was that Lilias had better go alone to see Margaret; but Lilias somewhat hastily negatived this proposal. It was an awkward visit to pay, and she would be glad of Marjory's assistance; she was afraid of speaking too frankly, and Marjory's presence would keep her in order : and so they went together.

But they were so late in starting that Mrs. Carr met them on her return from the Vicarage.

'You lazy girls !' she said, as she stopped to speak to them ; 'you have been talking instead of getting ready. It will be tea-time before you are back.'

' What did Mrs. Moore say, mother dear ?'

' Why, she is as angry as possible. She says Katie has behaved very badly. She has been engaged some time to Dr. Ainslie, only they have kept their own counsel. The children were always saying that they met Dr. Ainslie whenever they went out, and Katie was always running in to Margaret on some errand or other, but no one suspected anything ; it is all very unsatisfactory. Mrs. Moore says she is quite deceived in Katie; she thinks she has been very underhanded about this, and has shown herself extremely ungrateful. She has been quite a mother to her, and has taken such care of her. But now Katie complains of a pain in her side, and says she has been overworked, and she is sure it is this that has made Dr. Ainslie insist on such an early marriage.'

'Such nonsense!' broke out Lilias. 'I am sure Katie looks the picture of health.'

'Poor Mrs. Moore quite cried about it all! She said the Vicar was hurt, too, for they were all very fond of Katie. And do you know, Lilias, I am afraid she has not been perfectly open. She must have done more than drop a hint about Margaret, for Mrs. Moore said to me that she would be quite in despair at losing Katie, if Margaret were not coming to take her place with the children, at least for the present. Of course, I said nothing; but I do feel Katie has not been fair in this.'

Lilias gave a little shrug, and looked at Marjory.

'You were the only one who understood her,' she said frankly, as they walked on.

'Poor Margaret, I am afraid this is a sad business!'

Margaret turned very pale when she saw her visitors, but she greeted them quietly. Marjory, who had caught sight of her first, had been struck by her listless attitude. Margaret was sitting by the fireless grate, with her hands clasped upon her lap, evidently doing nothing: her books were closed, and her spectacles laid aside, and her mild, short-sighted eyes had a troubled look in them.'

'This is very kind,' she said, in a low voice; 'but I suppose you have heard——'

'Yes, Katie told us. Oh, I am so shocked, Margaret—so sorry about it all; and so are mother and Marjory.'

'Please don't tell me what they think;' and here her lips trembled slightly. 'When a thing is settled, talking is no use; and if it be for my father's happiness——'

'But, Margaret, surely yours ought to be consulted too.'

'Oh, that is not the question;' and her grand head drooped a little. 'We are not sent into the world to work out our own happiness, but our own salvation and the salvation of others.

If my father wishes to marry again—if I am not sufficient for his comfort—well, it may be hard, perhaps—I do not say it is not a trial—but he knows what is best for himself, and it is my duty to submit.'

'But Miss Stallard!' ejaculated Marjory; 'how can Dr. Ainslie choose such a girl to be his companion and yours?'

A deep flush passed over Margaret's face.

'Please hush! it is not for me to question my father's choice. I have always been very fond of Katie, though our tastes are not the same. She is very amiable and pretty—do you not think so? A clever man like my father could not care for her if she were not as nice as possible. I am afraid I am not sufficiently generous about it—at least, he said so last night. She is young, and poor, and friendless, and the world is too heavy for her. Of course I ought to be glad to welcome her, poor little thing!'

'Margaret, I think it is you who are to be pitied,' observed Lilias gently. 'It will make such a change in your life; no—I am not saying anything unkind of Katie. It is better to leave those sort of things unsaid—hard words do no good. But it is you of whom I am thinking.

What should I have felt if anyone had come between my mother and me?'

Margaret smiled faintly.

'Oh, Lilias, we each have our idols, and then we get punished through our very love; but our cases are not alike. My father is not always with me; and now I shall be too busy to sit down and fret over what cannot be helped.'

'But you are always busy.'

'Oh, but there will not be a minute of my time unemployed now. What, have you not heard?' as Lilias thought it better to pretend ignorance. 'Mrs. Moore is in dreadful trouble about the poor children, and my father thinks it will be a good thing for me to offer my services, at least for a time.'

'But, Margaret'—rather dubiously—'are you sure that this will not interfere with your other work?'

'Perhaps it will,' she returned calmly. 'But I think it is better not to be self-willed even over one's work. If a neighbour is in trouble, it is surely my duty to help her; and then I can see my father wishes it. I have the evenings for my poor people—I shall not be wanted at home.' Here, in spite of her courage, the tears rushed to her eyes. 'My father will not miss me so badly—I mean, he will have a wife to see after his little comforts. Katie is an excellent manager. I should not like my poor people to suffer; and if there are all those little girls to teach, besides my two boys, there will be only my evenings free.'

'I know what it will be!' returned Lilias impetuously. 'You will overwork yourself, and then the world will lose a saint!'

'It will lose a very weak, foolish woman,' replied Margaret, with a sigh. 'Oh, what a blessed rest it would be just to get away from one's self for a little! How the old Adam sticks to one, in spite of all one's efforts. Lilias, dear, please do not talk any more about me and my miserable affairs. We must take what heaven sends us, with both hands, and do the best we can with it—grumbling never helped anyone yet. Now tell me all the Mavisbank news, and a little about Redlands, too, if you will.'

And she leant back in her chair, with such an exhausted look upon her face that Marjory took pity on her, and changed the subject quickly.

CHAPTER VII.

'MARJORY, I AM HERE.'

WHEN Hurrell heard this wonderful piece of news, he expressed his indignation in no measured terms.

'What an old fool the doctor must be, to be caught by that little smooth-haired chit of a girl! I always told my mother that she was too deep for my taste. What an affront to Margaret, a grand creature like that! You are my liege lady, Lilias; but after you, I do not believe Westmorland holds another woman to compare with her.'

'Now, if I had never returned from Peru,' observed Lilias, with a charming pout, 'I have no doubt you would have married Margaret.' Of course, she expected to be contradicted; but to her surprise Hurrell replied, with the frankness that was natural to him:

'No doubt it would have been so; Margaret and I were old playmates. When I was ten years old I made her a decided offer; I gave her half my worldly goods, a share of my marbles and some hardbake, on the express understanding that she was to be my wife, and do all my sums for me. I am not quite sure that I did not jilt her, when I transferred my grown-up affections to you. What do you say, Lilias?'

Lilias gave him an affectionate little smile, but she did not answer. She was too sure of him to be jealous. No doubts could mar her perfect faith in him; but all the same his speech troubled her. No girl quite likes to hear that there was a time when her image was not paramount in her lover's imagination; at one time in his life, Margaret, and not she, had been Hurrell's friend. She wondered a little curiously if Margaret ever remembered this childish episode; if the defection of her old playmate had given her pain; if any promissory scheme of happiness had been checked when the young squire began to haunt Mavisbank.

'If things were so, I should never find it out

from Margaret,' she thought; 'her large unselfish nature would sustain a martyrdom rather than make a demand. I have known her all these years, and I have never heard her ask anything for herself;' and in this she did justice to Margaret.

Only a faint glimmer of the truth ever came to Lilias—a shadowy suspicion that never vexed her by becoming reality. No one really guessed Margaret's secret but Marjory, who, in her own unhappiness, was very keen to detect trouble in another. But even she only deduced slight imaginary inferences.

Margaret's noble reserve baffled even Marjory. Neither she nor any human being knew of the conflict that Margaret fought that night when she knew Lilias had promised to be Hurrell Wentworth's wife. When it was past, and she had regained her lost calmness, she took down from the shelf a favourite book; it opened of itself at a page that looked defaced and stained, as though with tears, and then she read slowly the following stanza:

'That bitter night
I sat astonished, till the unmeaning light

Of dawn broke on my heart, and showed how bare
It was. The evening and the morning were
The first day of an empty life to me.
I rose, and set my window wide to the free,
Fresh east, and knelt as I was used. May He
Who loved us until death, forget the prayer
I prayed that day!'

'That was true!' she said with a sigh; but as she read on, something luminous, like a smile, lit up her pale face:

'I rose at length, and swept
My heart, and garnished it, and never wept
When all the precious things were laid away
Which might remind me of the summer day,
Now gone for ever. All the morning hours
The sun poured richly through the windows wide
Into the vacant rooms. I brought sweet flowers
And decked the house. "Let fragrant things abide
Even in the Chamber still, from which the guest
Is gone for ever. Here let sunshine rest,
And the glad breezes enter, laughing low
And treading soft. Then I shall come and go
Without this heavy sense of loneliness
Oppressing me. These simple guests will bless
The Haunted Chamber."'

And when she had read so far, knowing within herself the full meaning of this parabolic and lovely poem, she wrote with her pencil, upon the margin, a brief sentence from her old friend, Thomas à Kempis : 'When thou shalt come to this estate, that tribulation shall seem sweet, and thou shalt relish it for Christ's sake ; then think it to be well with thee, for thou hast found a paradise upon earth.' And with that she closed the book with a firm hand, as though she were shutting up some precious treasure that would lose fragrance by being exposed to the light of day.

Margaret was conscious of no heroism when she so resolutely put away from her all thoughts of private happiness, and set herself simply to fulfil the duties of the day. Neither did she weaken her lofty purposes by self-blame, or bitter censure on others.

When Hurrell, in his perfect honesty, had told Lilias of his esteem and admiration for his old playmate, and had added that jesting remark in which he accused himself laughingly of having jilted Margaret for her sake, he had no idea how deep that childish attachment of theirs had been on Margaret's part.

Until Lilias's arrival at Mavisbank, Hurrell had haunted the doctor's house, and Margaret had been a constant visitor at Redlands. The very frankness of Hurrell's friendship for her had blinded her eyes to the fact that his boyish fancy for her had merged into a passionate and absorbing affection for the fair-haired Lilias. It was long before Margaret found it out for herself.

Hurrell, in his masculine carelessness and blindness, never guessed at Margaret's bruised hopes. He had been very fond of Maggie once; he had told her everything, and made her his confidante after a brotherly fashion. Of course he admired her—a grand simple creature, with no selfishness and no littleness about her; but if he had ever made love to her, he had forgotten it entirely. Lilias had so bewitched him that even Margaret faded into the background. He had no unkind intentions. Hurrell never hurt the smallest and most helpless creature of God's creation without a sort of pang that loss of life was necessary: he would have been incapable of wounding a woman. Margaret knew this; forgave him wholly; honoured him above all men—though in intellect he was a pigmy beside a feminine giant—and loved Lilias more because Hurrell loved her than for her own sake. And then, because her faithful heart made any sort of change impossible, and once loving meant always loving with her, she set herself to fill up the meagre outlines of her life with other people's joys and sorrows. 'She would dwell at the gates of their happiness,' the humble creature told herself, 'not as a beggar, but as a free woman, rejoicing in their good gifts. We must be content with what heaven sends us,' she had said; and in saying it, she was not far from peace.

And now another trouble, differing in its intensity, but threatening the very root of her domestic peace, had come upon Margaret. Hurrell had failed her, but she had still her father; and what comfort there had been in that thought! But now she was to be no longer his sole companion. In all the world of living, breathing human beings, there was not one who looked to her for happiness, who felt her necessary to him; and oh the blinding anguish of this, 'None loves thee best.'

Margaret was fond of Katie—that is, she never refused to open her heart to anyone who seemed to need her affection; and the poor little friendless thing had seemed an object of pity.

But as time passed on, and she saw more of the girl, she was not blind to her faults.

'She is not in love with my father,' she said to herself sorrowfully; 'but she is poor and ambitious, and needs a home. And then she hates teaching; and she is like a kitten, she wants to be petted. Oh, there is no harm in her! She has only manœuvred in her little way to get what she wants. But when she comes here, it is I who will be in the way; it is Katie who will be jealous of me. If my father talks to me, well, she will not like that; she is not clever, and it is irksome to listen to two people talking over one's head. And she will not let me do anything for him; and I must sit with my hands in my lap, and my father's wife will wait upon him. Oh, it will be better—far better, to help Mrs. Moore, and my poor people, and anyone that wants me, than to sit there, and feel one's heart turning to bitterness. I will never pain my father by looking unhappy, or as though he had made a mistake. Other people will say that to him by their looks, but not his daughter.'

Margaret hinted at these resolutions she had formed when Marjory came to see her one evening about a week after Katie's engagement was known.

It was about three days before the wedding, and she had left Lilias at the Vicarage. They had taken some handsome gifts from Mavisbank—a silk dress from Mrs. Carr, and some beautifully embroidered handkerchiefs. 'For we must be good to her for Margaret's sake,' Mrs. Carr had said; and she knew the silk dress would embellish the girl's scanty wardrobe.

Katie's blue eyes sparkled with pleasure as she unfolded the silk breadths.

'Oh, how kind!' she exclaimed. 'Do you know, I was so naughty that I nearly cried because I had only one new frock; and that is the one I am to be married in the day after to-morrow. I was quite unhappy, for I knew poor mamma could not give me a trousseau; but Dr. Ainslie laughed at me, and said he was marrying me and not my frocks; but that is so like a man—they never think of details as we do. But oh!' interrupting herself, 'this silk is lovely; and as for those handkerchiefs,' pouncing on them in a kittenish way, 'they are fit for a princess!'

Marjory had cut short the little bride-elect's

raptures rather ruthlessly by taking her departure. She would not wait to see the handsome mantle that Mrs. Moore had provided, or the beautiful lace and embroidery that Mrs. Wentworth had sent. She was in no mood for Katie's affectations. She went away on some pretext or other, leaving Lilias behind her; and then an impulse drew her to the bow-windowed house where Margaret sat alone, puzzling herself over the problems of existence.

They sat and talked a little, and then Marjory said abruptly: 'I suppose you will be at the church, Margaret—I mean on Thursday?'

'Yes,' she returned quietly; 'my father wishes it. They are going to Grange for a fortnight. You must come and see me a great deal when I am alone. Oh, I forgot!' with an attempt at cheerfulness; 'I have promised Mrs. Moore to begin lessons with the children on Monday. Only my evenings will be free; and then I have my poor people to visit. Never mind, we shall meet somehow; and I like to be busy,' as though to check any pitying comments.

'You will never let me speak,' remonstrated Marjory, in a grumbling tone. 'You are so good and strong that you can live without sympathy. I wish you would let me say once for all how sorry I am for you.'

Margaret looked in her face with her gentle short-sighted eyes.

'If it will do you any good, Marjory, I will listen to you; but it will only give me pain, and just the sort of pain that I find it difficult to bear. When one cannot speak without blaming some one, it is so much wiser to be silent.'

'Oh, you are a saint, as Lilias says,' was Marjory's impatient rejoinder. 'I did not think there was a woman living who could do without sympathy.'

'You are quite right,' returned Margaret, speaking with effort; 'no one can do without it. I am quite sure of my friends' affection for me. I never valued their kindness so much as I do now. They would be my friends still more if they would preach cheerfulness to me, instead of trying to weaken my strength.'

'Of course, I see what you mean,' reluctantly.

'Do you not see the wisdom of the homely old proverbs, "It is ill crying over spilt milk," and "Least said is soonest mended"? It is such a waste of words, just lamenting over what is not to be remedied. It is as idle comfort as the wailing of hired mourners round Jewish tombs. A real friend would help one to look one's trouble boldly in the face. I think that is what I would do in a similar case.'

'But your days will be so difficult to live,' lamented Marjory, who knew now, by sad experience, what it meant to wear the galling yoke of a strange trouble.

'Days are made up of hours and minutes,' returned Margaret, with a smile that was more pathetic than tears. 'There is one blessing, we can only live one minute at a time, after all,' with a wistful look. 'We are only like little birds, pecking out of our Father's hand a crumb here and a crumb there; and "not even a sparrow——" You know the rest, Marjory.'

'Dear Margaret, if we could all be like you, and live above our troubles!' burst from the girl's lips, as she rose to take her leave.

But Margaret only shook her head a little sadly. The gallant swimmer who is still breasting the deep waters is only conscious of effort and the coldness of the receding waves, and scarcely sees the stars above his head.

Marjory walked thoughtfully towards Mavisbank. The early glory of summer lay round her, but she scarcely heeded it. The bleating of the young lambs and the lowing of calves from the Castle Farm fell idly on her ear. The problematic troubles of existence occupied her—the difficulty of adjusting other people's lives according to one's sense of fitness.

She was just turning in at the gate of Mavisbank, when a red-headed urchin, who was loitering about the road, suddenly accosted her.

'Is your name Deane?' he asked abruptly, fixing a pair of wide-open blue eyes on Marjory, about as luminous and intelligent as a baby-calf's.

'Yes,' said Marjory as abruptly; but she coloured, as she always did now, at the falsity of her claim to that name. 'Who are you, my boy, and what do you want with me?'

'I am Georgie Patterson, and I live down at Moreland's Cottages. Here's summat for you, if your name is Deane.'

And he thrust a limp-looking paper in Marjory's hand, rather untidily folded; but as she opened it curiously, the sight of the well-known handwriting made her heart beat with a sickening prevision of coming difficulty.

'Marjory,' she read, 'I am here. You have promised me solemnly that you would come to me if I were dying. There are not many hours longer for me in this miserable world, so you must not fail me. The boy will tell you where I am at present.

'Miriam Chard.'

'The woman as sent me,' observed the boy, who was too busy fingering the marbles in his pocket to notice Marjory's evident emotion, ' is Miss Atkinson, living down in Moreland's Cottages. There is a lady with her that sent the note.'

'Will you take me to Moreland's Cottages?' interrupted Marjory, turning to him quickly.

She must go to her—that was her only thought. If they missed her at the dinner-table, well, that could not be helped. The only idea she could grasp was, that Mrs. Chard was here at St. Kilda's, that she was dying, and that the proofs of her real parentage were in her hands. There was not a moment to be lost.

She knew Miss Atkinson's name well. She was a distant connection of Mrs. Chard's—a respectable little dressmaker, who supported herself and a crippled sister. Her one source of perplexity was, how had Mrs. Chard managed to drag herself all these hundreds of miles in a dying state?

Marjory walked fast, for her thoughts were as tormenting as a gadfly; and in a few minutes they had reached Miss Atkinson's neat little house, which was distinguished from the neighbouring cottages by its trim flower-borders and bee-hives, and the white curtains that festooned the windows.

Miss Atkinson opened the door to them. She was a kind, black-eyed little woman, and had the bumps of benevolence and loquacity very strongly developed. She eyed Marjory a little doubtfully. She was not in her cousin's confidence, and could not be sure that the stylish-looking young lady before her was the Marjory who was Robert Deane's daughter. She had questioned her a little on the subject, and had been answered peevishly that she had no daughter now, and would not think of claiming one. Marjory had been as good as lost to her since the day she ran away.

'She has been asking a dozen times if you were not in sight,' began Miss Atkinson, with a mournful shake of her head. 'She is terribly bad and restless. I have had an awful time with her since she came last Monday. "I am a dying woman, Susan," she said to me that night, "but I made up my mind that I would be buried alongside of father and mother in St. Kilda's churchyard; and so I thought, being cousins once removed, you would take me in and do for me, like a good Samaritan." But there, Miriam was always a grand talker, and used longish words when short ones would have done. She has had a fine eddication—not that that matters when we come to die.'

'Is she in bed?' asked Marjory, hoping to check this flow of words.

'Well, no. Yesterday she was faint-like all the day, and scarcely stirred or spoke; but since morning she has been restless, and nothing will do but she must get up and sit by the fire. Dr. Ainslie says we may just humour her—it is only a flicker-like before the candle goes out. But for restlessness, she won't suffer, he says; which is a blessing, poor soul! for she has had her share of Adam's pain, if any woman ever had.'

'Will you let me go to her, please?' returned Marjory, with the touch of hauteur she knew so well how to assume.

Miss Atkinson wiped her eyes, and led the way up the narrow stairs, and ushered her into the small but spotlessly-clean room, with the evening sunshine streaming through the lattice-window on a red earthenware bowl full of wild flowers—pink and white briar roses and bunches of meadow-sweet.

Marjory felt a sudden shock of pity and repugnance as she caught sight of the wasted creature sitting pillowed-up in the chintz-covered chair, in the same grey wrapper in which she had seen her last; but as Mrs. Chard turned her haggard face towards her, and Marjory saw the sunken, miserable eyes and the pinched features, nothing but pity remained.

'You see, I sent for you, dearie,' she said in a weak voice, as Marjory took her hand. 'You may leave us, Susan; I want to talk to this young lady. Now, sit down, Marjory; for there is that I must say to you, and little time remains for me to say it in. You were hard with me last time we met, but I am not blaming you for that, for you had a deal to put up with and forgive; but I won't be an encumbrance much longer. In a few days you will have it your own way, and then, perhaps, your thoughts of me will be less bitter.'

'They are not bitter now,' returned Marjory gently; for even the old fretful voice aroused her compassion, it had grown so thin and weak; and as for the poor shrunken face, she would hardly have known it. How could she feel resentment against this crushed and bruised human being? 'I am sorry, very sorry to see you like this. How could you travel all these miles? Good heavens! you might have died on the way.'

'No, dearie, no,' she replied faintly; 'the breath could not leave my body while this longing was upon me. The wish was too strong upon me for that. A Whitecliffe neighbour was going on to Glasgow, and she travelled with me a bit. When they told me I hadn't many days to live, I could not stay there to die, with the sea roaring in my ears. I would be buried by mother and father. It was nothing to me that Ephraim was at Whitecliffe. If it had been Robert, now—but no, I thought I could rest best next to mother. And then there was that longing that seemed to parch me like thirst.'

'What longing?' asked Marjory, leaning forward; for she could hardly hear the weak tones.

'Nay, Marjory, you must know, surely. Isn't it to see my Lilias that I have dragged my half-dead body all these miles? You won't be vexed with me, dearie; for nothing will satisfy a mother but her own child. You will bring her to me to-night, will you not? I must see her sweet face again—so like my Robert's—and then I will gladly lie alongside of mother; for this world has been nought but a muddle to me.'

'How am I to bring her?' exclaimed Marjory, in a frightened tone. 'What am I to say to her?' And then she continued entreatingly, 'Will it not distress her to see you like this? Lilias is not strong, and she feels so deeply about things. I will stop with you, Mrs. Chard—I will do all I can to comfort you; but Lilias!—and if you should betray yourself!'

A quick, irritable look came into the dim eyes as Marjory said this. The obstinacy of the weak creature showed itself as she pushed the girl from her with trembling, impotent wrath.

'You—you!' she panted. 'When I want my child—you who have hated me all your life! Oh, I am not dying yet! If you will not bring her to me, I will crawl up there—if it be on my hands and knees, and though I were to die on the very threshold her dear feet have crossed!' And then she broke into miserable sobs, and put her hands together as though she were praying. 'Oh, you will not be so cruel, Marjory! There, dearie, I did not mean to be cross. All the papers are here'—touching her bosom. 'When the breath has gone out of me, you may take them, and then the power will be in your own hands. I have made it up to you as well as I could, Marjory; and you have been brought up a lady, and had the best of educations, and people have made much of you. I have only kept you out of your rights until you were a fine young woman, with all your life before you, and mine—done—done! But '—her voice becoming feeble again—' you will bring her, Marjory, if it is only for the sake of your own mother who bore you?'

Marjory covered her face at this appeal.

'Yes,' she whispered at last, ' I will bring her this very evening, if she will come with me.'

'Oh, she will come,' was the confident answer; 'she will come, my precious, if she hears her old nurse Miriam is dying, and wants to see her. Keep my mistress—keep Mrs. Carr from me, if you can; and now, Marjory, you and me have talked enough. Ask Cousin Susan to come to me, for I must have something to keep the life in me till she comes. Go, and don't be long; for I am that restless, that I feel I could fly through the window, for all I have not the strength of a baby!'

And Marjory, alarmed at the sudden greyness that crossed her face, sought Miss Atkinson without a moment's delay; and then with a troubled heart set out for Mavisbank.

CHAPTER VIII.

'LIFE'S FITFUL FEVER O'ER.'

THERE was a general exclamation when Marjory made her appearance in the dining-room, still in her walking-dress, and looking pale and disturbed; she had prepared her little speech beforehand, and now rehearsed it without a pause.

'I am so sorry to be late, but I had a sudden message to go down to Moreland's Cottages. Mrs. Chard is there, with her cousin, Miss Atkinson; she is very ill—dying. I do not think she can last more than a day or two.'

'Oh, Marjory!' exclaimed Lilias, with tears in her eyes, while Mrs. Carr took the girl's hand and pressed it. Hurrell and Barry were regarding her with grave looks of commiseration. A great lump rose in Marjory's throat;

she released her hand impatiently, and looked from one to the other with a little defiance. What was it to her that this woman lay dying? Had she not robbed her of her rightful inheritance, and made her existence a living lie?

'Oh, you need not be sorry for me!' she said proudly. 'It is Lilias that she is wanting to see. I am nothing to her—there is no love between us.'

'My dear, my dear!' observed Mrs. Carr in a shocked voice, while Hurrell looked uncomfortable, and seemed inclined to shift his place; but Lilias came up to the excited girl, and put her arms round her.

'Mother, never mind what she says. Hurrell, you do not understand. No one shall wrong Marjory by a thought. She is not to blame if she cannot love her mother. They have never lived together; of course there is no sympathy between them. Poor Miriam! of course she is sorry for her; but there are times when we cannot bear pity,' finished Lilias, in her warmhearted way.

'You are right,' returned Marjory, in a choked voice. 'I think if anyone pities me tonight I shall go mad!' And again there were compassionate glances exchanged. 'It is Lilias she wants to see,' she went on, forcing herself to be calm. '"There is no time to be lost!" —that is what she keeps saying.'

'My darling, it will only upset you,' observed Mrs. Carr anxiously. 'I will go myself— Marjory shall take me. You will wait, my dear, will you not, while I put on my bonnet? And Lilias, you must see that Marjory eats something. Her hands are cold, in spite of the warm evening—that is exhaustion from want of food. Oh, I shall not be long.'

But Marjory took hold of her, with appealing looks.

'Oh, please let Lilias go!' she said quickly. 'We must not disappoint dying people; and it was Lilias for whom she asked. "When she knows that her old nurse Miriam is dying, she will come and see me." Was not that what she said? Oh Sissie, you will not refuse to come with me, will you?'

'Of course I must go, mother!' cried Lilias impetuously. 'No, Hurrell; you are not to speak. What harm will it do me to see my old nurse again? Mother, please see to poor Marjory. You are right—she must eat something.'

And without waiting for an answer, Lilias ran out of the room, and returned in a moment with a black lace shawl arranged as a mantilla over her white dress.

Marjory was taking a little soup; but she pushed away her plate after a few mouthfuls.

'It is no use—I cannot take food just now,' she said rather irritably. 'Come, Sissie, I am ready!'

In her overwrought, nervous state, any form of kindness—any attention on her friends' part —seemed to bruise her sensibility. It vexed her when Mr. Wentworth accompanied them, as a matter of course, and still more when he announced his intention of waiting for Lilias. His few grave remarks were received by Marjory with impassive coldness. Why should they be kind to her, who was their worst enemy? In a few days she would have wrecked the happiness of that simple household. No; she could not accept their kindness to-night.

'Do not be long, dearest,' she could hear him say, as Lilias passed him on the threshold. 'You will find me walking up and down like a sentinel until you come out.'

Marjory brushed by them both with a sudden

impatient movement. She went upstairs, leaving Lilias to follow, and entered the sick-room.

'She is coming; I have brought her,' she said aloud; and then, stooping over Mrs. Chard, she almost hissed into her ear: 'Do not make me repent it. Be careful. You do not know how delicate and sensitive she is. For all our sakes, say nothing to make her suspect the truth. Leave that to me.'

'You may trust me, dearie,' gasped the invalid faintly. 'Lift me up on my pillows, Marjory. I am not so well to-night. Susan is fetching the doctor.' And then she stopped, and a sudden gleam came into the faded eyes, for Lilias was in the room, and the mantilla had fallen on her shoulders, leaving her fair hair uncovered; and what could be sweeter than her look, as she came up to the sick woman's chair and took her hand?

'My poor Miriam, you wanted to see me. My mother would have come—but no, Marjory would not bring her.'

'No, no; it was not the mistress I wanted—it was your sweet face I must see before I died. You are not afraid to kiss your old nurse, are you, my pretty?' And as Lilias stooped down and kissed her, the poor creature burst into weak tears.

'Oh, that was like heaven!' she sobbed. 'How many years is it since you kissed me? Not since you were a little child, when you would prattle for the hour together to your mammie—that was what you called me then. It is only my fancy, dear. You will humour your poor nurse who is dying; but if I could hear you say "mammie" once again!'

'Do it to please her, Sissie,' implored Marjory, touched to the heart by this little scene.

The mere presence of her child, the touch of her soft warm hands, seemed to infuse new life into the dying woman. Her eyes shone with joy and tenderness as Lilias knelt beside her, chafing the thin fingers, and looking at her with those clear compassionate glances. She was so accustomed to be loved that the affection of her old nurse did not seem to surprise her. 'Everyone was good to her,' thought Lilias, 'and why not this poor Miriam?'

'You are not suffering, dear mammie?' she said quite naturally, speaking, as she thought, a child's pet-name. 'Why do you tremble so? Shall I put my arm round you to support you?

Is there anything we can give her, Marjory? She looks so exhausted.'

But Marjory shook her head. She knew Lilias was giving her the only cordial that could revive her.

'It is like heaven!' sighed the invalid again; and as Lilias supported her, her hair brushed softly against Mrs. Chard's face.

Marjory felt a strange contraction of heart as she saw how the dying lips tried to touch it.

'Kiss her once more, Sissie dear,' she said, hardly knowing that she spoke, only the words escaped her.

And Lilias, wondering a little, obeyed her.

'But you must kiss her too, Marjory,' she said, looking up rather tearfully; 'Miriam—mammie I mean—we must not forget our poor Marjory.'

A long shiver passed over the sick woman's frame.

'No; we will not forget her,' she murmured. 'Let bygones be bygones, dearie; and though there is much to forgive, there is mercy in heaven, and why not on earth? Let me see you beside her, my two darlings that you were—Marjory and Sissie, Sissie and Marjory.'

Here her poor brain became confused, and she went on incoherently :

'My girl and hers. But Sissie has Robert's eyes, and she has my long face; but her hair is shining gold like an angel's.'

'Lilias!' cried Marjory, rising to her feet in sudden alarm; 'you must not stop. She is very ill—very. You must go down and find Miss Atkinson.'

But Lilias refused.

'She has gone for Dr. Ainslie. I cannot leave you alone, Marjory. There is death in her face. And oh, you poor woman! what is it you have to say to me?'

But Marjory thrust herself between them, and almost pushed her away.

'Go down to Mr. Wentworth. He must tell them to be quick—very quick. Lilias, you must not stay. She is wandering; and there are things that only I have a right to hear.' Then, stooping down, she touched Mrs. Chard's lips with her hand. 'For Lilias—oh, remember it is for Lilias!' she said, trying to arrest the poor creature's restless flow of words. But the clouded brain refused to take in the full meaning of Marjory's speech.

'Yes, yes—you are right. She is my baby; and we called her Lilias out of love to my young mistress. Why do you come between us, Marjory? One hair of her head is dearer to me than your whole body.'

'Lilias!' remonstrated Marjory, white with fear; 'you are only exciting her. See how her poor mind is wandering! Let me take your place, and ask Mr. Wentworth to bring the doctor.'

And Lilias, confused by the invalid's sudden incoherence, and alarmed by her sunken looks and laborious breathing, rose at once.

'Good-bye, my poor Miriam!' she said, stroking the cold face. But the feeble hands held her fast.

'She has Robert's eyes,' she gasped; 'but we will not tell her so. No, no, no, Marjory; we will do nought to harm her—you and me. Cover me up, dearie, for I am cold, and the sea seems in the room somehow;' and her voice became weak and almost inaudible.

The next moment Marjory was left alone. Lilias's emotional nature could no longer endure the scene. Her face was pallid, and the tears were streaming down her face as Hurrell came towards her.

'Oh, it was terrible!' she said, clinging to his arm. 'She did not know what she was saying, and she took me for Marjory. Poor Miriam! she was thinking of her own child, not of me. She wanted me to kiss her again and again. She thought I was her baby. She was fond of us both. She has been good to me all my life; but, of course, she must have taken me for Marjory.'

'This has been too much for you,' he said very tenderly, making her lean on him; for she trembled from head to foot. 'Your mother was right. You ought not to have come.'

'We cannot refuse the dying,' she returned gently.

And then he said no more—only waited patiently until she had recovered herself.

As they stood there in the fading light, they had no idea that at that moment a sorrowful soul was passing. Lilias had hardly crossed the threshold, before Marjory, to her horror, saw that mysterious grey veil settling upon the worn face—that veil which is never to be lifted in this world; and, with an instinctive longing to give comfort at that dread moment, she gathered the dying woman's hand in hers, and repeated softly those sacred words:

'"Yea, though I walk through the valley of the shadow of death, I will fear no evil: for Thou art with me; Thy rod and Thy staff they comfort me."'

Was it fancy that a dim shadowy smile came on the poor face? Marjory would always have it so. In her own mind she had no doubt that the Divine Shepherd was carrying His bruised and weary sheep most safely through that dark valley. What if she had wandered into devious ways, and had torn herself against the cruel brambles, and fallen into many a pitfall? Had not the weak soul cried oft and bitterly for help and deliverance? Her sins were many; but who could doubt the mercy of the All-merciful —that He was taking His lost and sorely troubled child home to rest?

There were footsteps approaching — Dr. Ainslie's and Miss Atkinson's—and at the sound Marjory hastily drew from the dead bosom the sealed packet that had lain there night and day for the last week, and thrusting it hurriedly into her dress, turned away from the bed.

She was almost as pale as the corpse as she answered the doctor's few inquiries.

'I do not know. I have never seen anyone die before,' she said, as he asked her if the poor creature had passed without a struggle. 'Her mind seemed confused when Lilias was here. She went back to the past, when we were little children. I told Lilias to go, for she was exciting her; and then I saw the look on her face. It frightened me, and I said a verse to comfort her; and then she smiled—oh, quite happily, but so strangely! and then——'

Marjory shuddered and turned away. She was young, and she had never seen death; and to be alone with it!—it was a new and terrible experience. She could not speak of it.

Dr. Ainslie took her arm and led her gently from the room. Outside, the two lovers were talking softly to each other under the waning light. A star or two shone in the summer sky, a faint crescent moon hung behind the trees.

'Take them home,' he said, speaking to Hurrell. 'The poor woman up yonder is dead. There is nothing more to be done for her.'

'Oh, Marjory, and I left you alone!' exclaimed Lilias remorsefully.

Marjory tried to move her dry lips in answer, but her voice seemed gone. She hardly knew that Mr. Wentworth had come round to her side, and had given her his arm, and that Lilias walked beside them. Her limbs moved stiffly; a sort of stupor of insensibility seemed over her. Death!—then this was death, and she had seen it with her own eyes; and why was she repeating that clause over and over to herself, 'As we forgive them that trespass against us'? Forgive! Oh yes; she had forgiven her now!

'The shock has been too much for her,' observed Hurrell, in a low voice. 'Oh, how I wish your mother had gone!'

His words roused Marjory.

'I cannot see her to-night,' she said a little wildly, clutching Lilias's arm. 'Let me go to my room. I can see no one to-night. Promise me that I shall see no one — no one!'

'You shall be as quiet as you like, dear,' returned Lilias soothingly; and the next moment they had reached Mavisbank, and Marjory, with a brief 'Good-night,' had passed quickly through the hall before Mrs. Carr's voice could reach her.

Marjory was fleeing for refuge to her own room, like some hunted creature that had got a deadly hurt. The crisis of her life had approached, and she knew it. The dead hand had unsealed her lips; the secret need no longer be kept.

She locked her door, and then, throwing off her hat—for a fever seemed upon her—she lighted her candle and sat down by the open window. In the dim twilight the dark foliage of the Mavis Woods was plainly visible, like a sombre screen shutting out the world; but the mysterious aspect outside failed to disturb her.

She had broken the packet, and was reading, devouring rather, the record of a woman's duplicity. Clear and simple and sorrowful was the statement—not one point omitted, not one clue lost. The feeble mind that had dictated every word had at least been sincere in its repentance.

Only one paper was left unopened — an envelope directed to Mrs. Carr, and under the name was faintly scrawled, 'To my deeply wronged mistress, from her repentant servant, Miriam Chard.'

Marjory folded them all together, and then stood for a moment looking out into the eerie darkness.

'Ah, you poor soul!' she murmured, 'you have left it to me—the bitter work of unravelling this miserable plot; but I forgive you—yes, as there is a heaven above us both, I forgive you fully and freely.'

When she had said this, some of the intolerable load seemed removed from her heart, and she could think more calmly.

When Lilias came to her door presently with the sorely needed refreshments, she did not refuse them, but thanked her in her old manner, and sent her love to Mrs. Carr, and begged that they would not trouble about her any more to-night.

'But you will go to bed when you have had your supper?' coaxed Lilias, a little uneasy at the strained look in Marjory's eyes.

'Yes, when I have written to Anne,' returned Marjory quietly. 'I cannot sleep just yet. Please do not stay, Lilias; I shall be better left to myself.'

And Lilias went away a little sorrowfully, and told the others 'that Marjory looked so very, very unhappy, only she was not crying, and did not seem able to bear a word.'

The food had arrived opportunely, for Marjory had felt a sinking that seemed to rob her of all strength. But when she had drunk the coffee, and eaten a little, she was able to write her letter. She concocted it carefully, and Anne, when she read it, failed to detect any trace of emotion in the writer. She thought Marjory might have shown a little more feeling about the poor creature.

'It is all over, and I cannot pretend to grieve,' wrote Marjory. 'Our unnatural relation to each other forbids any show of sorrow on my part. I feel more kindly to her than I have ever done; she is sacred to me now;' and so on through the calmly-worded letter.

'She says nothing about coming home, you see,' observed Anne, as she read it aloud to her brother.

It had not reached her until the evening of the day that made Katie Stallard Dr. Ainslie's wife, and on the following morning Mrs. Chard was to be buried.

'It is a very long letter, and tells us everything but the one thing I long most to know.' Anne raised her face, and looked at Capel wistfully—it had grown somewhat worn and delicate, and there were anxious lines on the forehead.

'She has written on the night it occurred,' he returned quietly; but his hand trembled slightly as it touched the paper. 'Her mind is full of that, and of nothing else. Do not look so sad, Anne, my dear; you will soon get your child back.'

'But, Capel,' she said imploringly, and now the tears came into her gentle eyes, 'will you not change your mind, now, about going away? Marjory may need you; you cannot tell how things will be, or if——' but here she paused, for he was looking at her now with a terrible sadness in his eyes.

'I must go all the sooner that this has occurred,' he answered quickly. 'She will come home—I know she will. And, Anne, you may call me an old fool, anything you like—I shall deserve any name—but I cannot stay to see her. How could I go on living day after day with her in the house, knowing there was no hope for me?'

'No, dear, no!' she faltered; 'it would be too hard for you. You could not bear such a struggle. Forgive me, Capel, and I will try not to be selfish over it any more; but you are my only brother!' and a tear rolled down her face.

'Poor Anne!' he said remorsefully; 'I give you nothing but trouble. Shall I stay and try my best to bear it? Will this please you, you small woman?'

He spoke with forced cheerfulness, but there was no mistaking the expression of his haggard face.

'Dear Capel, no,' she returned, drying her eyes, and taking up her work again. 'I would not keep you here for worlds; it will do you harm; it would not be for your good. You shall go; I will not say another word to hinder you. Only, Capel, try and feel better about it all, and then you can come back to me again.'

'I will promise that,' he replied gravely. 'You are a good woman, Anne—a little saint! There is not a man living who is fit to kiss the hem of your garment; men are such cowards, my dear. They cannot stay at home and brood over their worries; it would drive them mad.

Take care of her for me, and both of you say your innocent prayers and live in peace; and when I have grown wiser and stronger I will come back to you, and never leave you again.'

CHAPTER IX.

'YOU WILL SPEAK OPENLY TO ME?'

TO a psychologist—that is, one versed in the nature and properties of the soul—to anyone conversant with the phenomena of the mind, there would have been something pathetic and altogether pitiful in the crude girlish workings of Marjory's thoughts that night.

An 'infant crying in the dark' could not have groped about with more helpless hands and dim tear-stained eyes than Marjory, as, unaided and alone, she sought to solve the problem that lay before her.

Over and over she repeated to herself that she had arrived at the crisis of her life. Her painful secret need no longer be preserved; truth demanded a full and immediate revelation. No one could keep her out of her rights—those precious rights of a mother's and brother's love. Why should she continue to live a falsehood? Why should she, Lilias Marjory Carr, be known a moment longer as Marjory Deane, the blacksmith's daughter? And yet, as she told herself all this, Marjory trembled and wept.

To her generous and affectionate nature there was anguish in the thought that her happiness must be built on the wreck of another's peace. How would Lilias bear such a bitter trial? Would not her sensitive and delicate organization shrink and wither under the shock? 'Oh, I must be careful, or it will kill her!' thought Marjory, feeling within herself a foretaste of Lilias's agony.

Then there sprang up in the girl's mind one of those quick impulsive inspirations that were natural to her. She would not break her news suddenly. She would dress up the truth in the semblance of fiction. She would concoct a little story that should shadow forth reality; and she would tell it to them, her mother and Lilias, as they sat together. She would plead her cause in this way; and then gradually, very gradually, the truth should unfold itself. But first, there was a question that she must put to Dr. Ainslie; and at this point she remembered that the next day—for already the morning was breaking on her vigil—would be his wedding-day. There was no time to be lost. She would rise early, and go to his house before she met the others at breakfast. What was the loss of a little sleep? Nothing could make her ill, she thought, with a mixture of self-scorn and pity. And so she wove out her simple plot, never asking herself if she would have strength to carry it out. Marjory was making her third great mistake. Her first error was when a dread of consequences induced her to give that promise of secrecy to Mrs. Chard. Her second was entering her rightful home as a stranger; and now her pride and impulse were carrying her away. It never entered her head to consult those true friends who had watched over her life, and who would have aided her in this emergency. She shrank from the idea of asking Mr. Frere's counsel. It was her own affair, she told herself. No one should interfere between her and her mother; but in this her girlish sophistry led her into grievous errors.

Poor impetuous misguided girl! yet surely

representative of the young generation that are wise in their own eyes, and, refusing ancestral lamps, prefer their own paltry rushlights, carrying them with youthful unguarded enthusiasm into the damp murky vaults they seek to explore. What wonder if they are blown out, and there is the loud bitter cry of an Esau-like repentance.

The faint twittering of birds was plainly audible from the Mavis Woods, and the first streak of daylight was in the east, when Marjory, after refreshing herself by ablutions and change of dress, lay down for an hour or two, until it was time to go to Dr. Ainslie. She slept heavily, and only woke when Emma entered her room.

The girl looked frightened when she saw Marjory stretched outside the coverlet in her usual morning dress.

'Oh, miss! to think of your never having been to bed!' she exclaimed, in a horrified voice. 'And you dressed, and looking so poorly too!'

'But I am not ill,' returned Marjory, sitting up and pushing back her heavy hair from her hot face. 'Have you brought me a cup of tea,

Emma? Thank you! that was very thoughtful. My head does ache a little; but I shall drink this and go out, and the cool air will do me good. Please do not tell anyone that you found me like this. If one cannot sleep, there seems no use in going to bed.'

'Very well, miss,' replied Emma doubtfully, but her round good-tempered face wore an uneasy expression. 'She do look mortal bad, to be sure,' she said to herself as she withdrew. 'There's more than a headache that ails her— I'll take my oath of that. But there, what is the good of trying to find out other folks' worries?'

Marjory was compelled to endorse Emma's opinion when she caught sight of her pale face and heavy eyes. 'Dr. Ainslie will think I am ill too,' she thought. I must go up Scarsgill and let the morning air freshen me up a little. I never saw myself before with this leaden complexion.' And accordingly, her strong will compelled her aching limbs to climb up the woodland paths to breezy Scarsgill; and then she sat down on a fragment of rock, and resolutely keeping thought at bay, let the fresh breezes blow over her face, until she felt she dared brave the doctor's keen eyes.

She found him working in the little front garden. It was one of his hardy habits to dig and hoe his flower-borders and vegetable beds before idle folk thought of stirring. It was good for the muscles and brain, he always said.

He gave a low whistle of surprise as Marjory unlatched the gate.

'You are out betimes, Miss Deane,' he said, with a quick glance through his spectacles. 'Do you want Maggie? She is in the kitchen, making the porridge for our breakfast. Maggie's porridge beats Sarah's. No one makes porridge like Maggie.'

'No; I want to speak to you a moment, Dr. Ainslie. There is a question I must ask; but I have not come to see Margaret.'

'Come to my study,' he returned, throwing down his hoe and leading the way into the house.

Margaret was singing a German hymn, in her deep voice, as she moved across the red-tiled floor, 'Ein feste Burg ist unser Gott.' Marjory caught her breath for a moment as she listened.

'Well,' observed Dr. Ainslie kindly, as he

placed a chair for her, 'what is this question?'

His professional eye had noted at once the girl's paleness and harassed looks. He thought she had come to consult him about herself, but her next words undeceived him.

'Dr. Ainslie, you will think it very strange—will you not?—but I want to speak to you about Lilias—Miss Carr, I mean. I am not quite easy about her health.'

'Indeed!'

Dr. Ainslie's manner changed in a moment. He seemed on his guard, and entrenched in professional reserve. Marjory understood at once that her errand surprised him, and that he was not prepared to talk over his patients with a stranger.

All this was patent to Marjory, though he only uttered that dry 'Indeed!'—but his lifted eyebrows spoke volumes.

'You must not think me impertinent, or interfering in other people's business,' faltered Marjory, with an appealing look. 'If I had not a very good reason for speaking to you on such a subject, I should hardly venture to question you. Dr. Ainslie, may I be frank with you—

that is—I mean '—hesitating over her words—
' will my confidence be safe with you ?'

' My dear young lady, I hope so,' in a half-affronted tone. ' Doctors are almost confessors in their own way.'

' Oh, you must not be offended with me !' she pleaded in an innocent, childish manner that touched him. ' If you knew how unhappily I am placed, you would do all you can to help me. I will tell you what I can, but that is not much. I am not speaking as a stranger. I love Lilias, and I would do anything I could to save her pain—that is, almost anything,' interrupting herself.

' Well, well,' he returned a little impatiently, ' what is it you want to know ?'

' It is just this,' speaking in a trembling voice. ' There is something I have heard—that I know—some bad news—that is, that she will consider it bad news—which will, I am afraid, give her a severe shock. No one knows it but myself and—and—the woman who is dead.'

' Do you mean the woman who died last night—Mrs. Chard ?' he asked, looking at her keenly. Indeed, he may be pardoned if a strong feeling of curiosity impelled him to ask this question.

Marjory bowed her head in assent.

'And it is bad news?' he continued.

'Very bad news to Lilias. Oh, I cannot tell you what it is! I must not—I dare not; but it will make her so unhappy. Oh, I am afraid it will almost break her heart!' and here Marjory's lips grew white and dry as she spoke.

'Is it in your power to withhold this news— I mean, would it be right to do so?' watching her intently.

'I suppose it would be in my power not to speak,' she replied, after a moment.

'But would it be right to do so?' he persisted.

'I cannot answer that question,' she returned, with a painful flush. 'How do I know what is right and wrong until you answer me? Dare I venture to speak, under Lilias's present condition of health? She is not strong. Once or twice she has alarmed me.'

'No, she is not strong,' he answered slowly. 'I spoke to her mother the other day. I gave her a hint, but I dared not speak openly. Those two seem bound up in each other.'

'But you will speak openly to me?' she pleaded. 'Think of the harm I might do if I were not cautious.'

'It will be needful for you to be cautious,' he returned significantly. 'She is very emotional—very.' He seemed deliberating with himself, for after a minute or two he continued very slowly: 'Perhaps, after all, it might be a dangerous experiment. If it be in your power to keep silence, Miss Deane, and if it would not be wrong to do so, I would almost advise that course.'

Marjory shivered.

'I must think it over. I cannot promise to do that. Indeed, I fear the truth must be told; but I will be careful. I will not speak suddenly. I will open her eyes by degrees—I——'

'Miss Deane,' he said suddenly, 'I wish you would confide in me. Your manner alarms me. Indeed, I must warn you—Miss Carr has heart disease.'

'Do you mean that any shock would be dangerous?'

'There would be always risk,' he returned evasively. 'If they take care of her—if she is saved too much worry, she may live as long as any of us. One can never judge in this sort of case; so much rests with the patient. Miss Carr is emotional, excitable; her spirits wear out her strength. I thought it right to warn her mother, and I told her Hurrell ought to have a hint given him. But there! women are such difficult subjects. Mrs. Carr only cried, and begged he might not be told; he knew already Lilias was delicate, and it would make him so unhappy.'

'Did you tell Mrs. Carr that Lilias had heart disease?' asked Marjory, regarding him with fixed, anxious eyes.

'Not in so many words. Better not—better not. What is the use of making people's lives a burthen to them? I said her heart was weak —that any form of excitement was bad for her; that was enough to say. In organic disease like that there is nothing that can be done. Why, she may outlive us both. But what beats me,' dropping his voice, 'is the fact of Mrs. Carr having two such sickly children. Of course, Philip Carr was not a strong man; but it is hard neither of them take after their mother.'

The same dark uncomfortable flush passed

over Marjory's face. She rose hastily, afraid lest the doctor's keen eyes should read her thoughts.

'Thank you. I know now that I am to be very, very careful. It shall be broken gently to Lilias. Oh, I will be very tender and careful with her!'

And then she held out her hand to the doctor, and said something about Margaret—that she sent her love, and could not wait to speak to her.

'Thank you,' she said again. 'You have spoken plainly to me, and I think it was right to do so. I wish I could have been as frank on my side, but it was not possible.'

'Everything is possible,' he answered, in some perplexity.

He was troubled within himself what all this might mean. What had this young stranger to do with the Carr household? How was it that she was possessed of some painful secret connected with them? It was impossible not to be impressed with her earnestness and restrained agitation. The good doctor shook his head, sorely puzzled, as he watched her go down the garden-path.

As for Marjory, an absolute blankness of thought seemed to possess her—an utter negation of idea, like the painlessness that sometimes occurs in a mortal hurt. A dull terror, that was almost despair, was creeping over her; but, with her strong will, she refused even to glance at the dark forebodings that seemed taking shape within her. She would be very careful, she told herself—very, very careful. She knew now what it was she had to fear. She would go over it point by point, patiently and minutely, before she hazarded the first step. A day or two's delay would not matter; that poor woman must be laid in her grave, and then—— But here Marjory could look no farther, for a numb, paralyzing force seemed to keep all anticipatory thought at bay.

Very little was said to Marjory during breakfast. Mrs. Carr was shocked and pained by the girl's immobility and changed looks. She and Lilias exchanged glances full of commiseration and pity—no one could accuse Marjory of want of feeling now.

Mrs. Carr left the girls together for the greater part of the morning, but there was little conversation between them. Marjory took a book and ensconced herself in the bay-window, but she did not once turn a page. Lilias, who had letters to write, came to her side once or twice with a caressing word or two; but Marjory hardly responded, and Lilias had gone back to her occupation.

Presently Mrs. Carr returned and sat down by Marjory. Her fine face looked a little saddened.

'My dear,' she said, in her usual kind voice, 'I hope that you do not think that I have left you alone too long. There were arrangements to make, and Miss Atkinson was glad of my assistance. It seems that poor Miriam had left full instructions with her cousin. She is to be buried as near her parents as possible, and her great wish is that you and my Lilias should follow her.'

Marjory made no answer.

'We think,' continued Mrs. Carr gently, 'that it will be as well to get it over as soon as possible; Dr. Ainslie advises it strongly, so we have fixed the funeral for the day after tomorrow. I do not know what we are to do about your mourning, Marjory. If you had a black dress, perhaps you might manage for the present——' But here she stopped; for a hard, sullen expression had come to the girl's face.

'I shall not wear mourning,' she said abruptly.

'My dear!'

'I will not be guilty of such hypocrisy!'—in an angry voice. 'Why should I pretend to grieve, when I have no such feeling in my heart? No, do not let us talk of this,' as Mrs. Carr seemed inclined to argue the point with her; 'not now—not for a day or two. I have a black dress; I will wear that for the funeral. I do not wish to be unseemly or show bad taste, but no one shall force me to put on mourning for her. She wronged me—she did me harm—but I hope I forgive her.' And here Marjory started up in strong agitation, and left the room; and for the rest of the day she hardly opened her lip s.

CHAPTER X.

'FOR LILIAS.'

IT was a hot, breathless June evening. All day long there had been an oppression and weight in the air, as of an impending storm. A margin of low, sullen-looking clouds fringed the horizon; in the Mavis Woods the birds were chirping restlessly in their nests; not the faintest breeze agitated the leaves —they hung motionless, waiting till the master-hand should play a windy symphony over them.

Mrs. Carr had tempted the two girls to an evening stroll. Barry, who always suffered much from the heat, had retired to his own room, complaining of neuralgic pains in his back and head; the suppressed electricity in the air made him nervous and irritable. Lilias, too, looked a little languid and depressed; the sad ceremony of the morning—for Mrs. Chard had been buried that day—had excited and tired her; her sympathy and pity had caused her to shed tears. But even the few stragglers in the churchyard had noticed the hard, stern look on Marjory's face, as she stood with downcast eyes by Lilias's side.

In spite of her kind heart, Mrs. Carr felt herself a little repelled and baffled by Marjory's strange manner. For the last two days she had eaten little, and had hardly spoken; she had moved among them with dry eyes, like one in a dream. That very morning, a letter had come from Murrel's End, and she had put it in her pocket unread. Once during the day she had reminded her of it.

'Yes, I know; it is from Anne. I will read it by-and-by,' she had said, almost indifferently; and there it still lay untouched in her pocket.

'You will come out with us, will you not?' Mrs. Carr had said, but she hardly expected that Marjory would be inclined to accompany them; but, to her surprise, she at once agreed.

She still wore her black dress; but half

absently, she took up a crimson silk handkerchief and tied it over her dark hair. Black did not suit Marjory, but the sudden relief of bright colour set her off to the best advantage. Mrs. Carr wondered at the bad taste, but held her peace; as for Marjory, she was perfectly unconscious of what she had done.

Lilias had led the way to her favourite seat; and Marjory, who had never visited that spot since the day Mr. Frere had spoken to her, felt a new pang at the sight of it. If only he were here to help her now, she thought, with a sudden yearning for that kindly face; and for the first time that day a mist gathered in her eyes.

Mrs. Carr and Lilias did not notice her softened expression. They were talking to each other; they both started when Marjory struck into their conversation. Lilias was speaking of a book she and Mrs. Carr had been reading. It had interested them greatly; and there was a character in it of a girl that Lilias declared might have been meant for Margaret.

'I know the book,' observed Marjory, trying to speak in her natural voice; 'but it is not by a good author. The end is tame and spiritless, compared to the beginning. Many of these stories are. It gives one the impression that the author has got tired of his or her work.'

'Perhaps they have left off building for want of materials,' suggested Lilias, 'like Mr. Andrews with those shabby cottages at the foot of Scarsgill; they always seem to want more finish.'

'I don't know about that,' returned Marjory. 'Now and then I have read a book that reminds me of some half-finished tenement with the scaffolding still up, just as though a sudden frost had hindered the workmen. There was a book that I read some time ago——' and then she stopped, for there was a strange lump in her throat that seemed to choke her.

'Yes, dear,' observed Lilias, in an interested voice, for she was pleased to hear Marjory talking in her old fashion, though to be sure her voice was a little husky.

'I think the author must have had a touch of frost too, or she must have been too tired to go on, for I know there was a dreadful muddle at the end. It seemed to be left to the readers to conjecture things as they liked.'

'What was its name, Marjory?'

'Oh, I cannot remember that!' she answered,

with an anxious catch of her breath; but they neither of them noticed how pale she had suddenly become. 'It was some time ago that I read it. It was true—that is, the facts had really happened, and the author had woven them into a three-volume novel. The strangest part to me, and what makes the terrible interest of the book, is that it is all true.'

'Why, Marjory, you speak as though it were a dreadful story!'

'No; I do not mean that; there were no murders or horrible things of that kind! It was only so very sad, and all the sadder because it was true, and the people really lived—indeed, are still living.'

'My dear, how could you know this?'

'Because the author is a friend of mine. But I cannot tell you the name! Oh no; that is how I know the characters are still living, and that it is all true and really happened; and it was called "Some one's Mistake" or "Atonement"—but it does not matter about the title!'

'Oh, but it does, you tiresome child!' returned Lilias, in her old merry voice. 'You have made me curious, and now I want to read it for myself. You must remember the name,

Marjory, or how am I to order it from Mudie's? "Some one's Mistake," or "Atonement." It will be dreadfully vague!'

'But it is out of print,' stammered Marjory. 'Perhaps you could not get it. And after all, it is very sad; and the people are living now, and they cannot all be happy. I will tell you a little about it, and then you will judge for yourself.' And then she began very slowly and hesitatingly her own story.

It seemed to Marjory as though she were speaking in a dream. Her own voice sounded metallic and unreal, and yet she was never so intensely alive to outward impression. She did not lose an expression on Lilias's face.

Hurrell's bench could only hold two people comfortably, so Lilias had spread a rug on the grass and sat at their feet, with her head resting against Mrs. Carr and her face turned to Marjory. As the story proceeded, she drew down Mrs. Carr's hands and laid her cheek against them, and presently a tear wetted them.

'Why, Lilias, you are crying! How absurd, when it is only a story!' observed Mrs. Carr presently.

'But, mother, it is true. Don't you remember Marjory told us so? The people are living to whom this dreadful thing happened. Oh, how sad it is! Marjory, I can hardly bear to hear you; there is something in your voice that makes me cry. Oh, that poor girl!'

'Which girl are you pitying?' demanded Marjory huskily; 'the one who has been kept out of her rights all these years, or the one who innocently supplanted her?'

'I do not know,' faltered Lilias; 'it was dreadful for the real daughter, of course. But then you remember, Marjory, that the other one —Lena, you call her, but I suppose that was not really her name—actually believed that she was living with her own mother, and that she idolized her;' and here she kissed the hand she held.

Mrs. Carr smiled, for she knew what inference Lilias had drawn.

'Yes, they simply idolized each other,' returned Marjory, in a strained voice. 'They had grown to each other all these years, until no flesh and blood relationship could be dearer. It seemed to the mother—at least the author told me so—that they thought alike, felt alike, and knew no happiness apart. It was a sort of elective affinity that dominated and superseded nature, for,' finished Marjory, with a break in her voice, ' there seemed no instinctive drawing of the mother's heart to her own child.'

'How very strange!' observed Mrs. Carr; 'and yet I do not know why I should say that. Of course, the mother and child were strangers; she had no presentiment of the truth.'

'But when it was told her?' asked Marjory, without raising her eyes to the calm beautiful face beside her.

'I do not know what any woman could do under such circumstances,' returned Mrs. Carr, in rather a troubled voice, for the suppressed passion in Marjory's low tones affected her as well as Lilias. 'I think it would almost break her heart to know that she had lavished all that love on another woman's child, and that in spite of herself the knowledge had come too late.'

'Do you mean that her heart would be closed to her own child? Oh no—impossible!' Marjory spoke as though the words were choking her.

'Not by her own will,' returned Mrs. Carr,

with a sigh. 'If she were a good woman, she would try to satisfy them both; but I think her heart—any mother's heart—must break over such an impossible task. Her own child would appear to her in the light of an interloper. She could not thrust away her adopted child, who had been her ewe lamb, and had lain so many years in her bosom. And it really happened, Marjory, and that poor woman is still alive? One must have thought that the pain and the worry would have fretted her into her grave long ago.'

'And you, Lilias?' asked Marjory hoarsely; 'what would you have done in Lena's place— the girl who was not the real daughter, you know?' but as she asked the question, Lilias raised herself to her knees, and cast her arms about her mother. She was trembling all over.

'Oh, mother, mother! can such things ever happen? How can they live through them? If I had been Lena, I should have died; I could not have lived a minute. What, lose my mother! Ask Marjory not to go on—her voice frightens me; and oh, the storm!' for here the first low peal of thunder seemed to roll and vibrate in the distance, and the oppression became still more intense and breathless.

'Come, dearest, or the storm will be upon us before we reach the house!' exclaimed Mrs. Carr anxiously.

Lilias was often hysterical at the approach of a storm, and there was some excuse that, in her desire to shield her child from nervous terror, she forgot the other girl, who was still sitting motionless in her place.

As the two figures hurried across the narrow dell, Marjory put up her hand to her throat. Were her senses leaving her? or why was she obliged to stifle the hoarse scream that seemed as if it must find vent? The next moment she wanted to break into loud laughter; how that bitter merriment would have scared the women who were hurrying through the wood, hand-in-hand! But she overcame that awful longing, holding herself by main force in her seat, while cold perspiration bedewed her forehead, and she shook as though in an ague fit.

Over her head the clouds were gathering more darkly: the sullen muttering of the thunder broke at intervals in her ears. Was Marjory quite cognizant of her own actions, when her cold hands drew from the folds of her dress the documents that were to prove her identity? Was there any conscious meaning in the reckless thought that prompted her to open the letter that Miriam Chard had written to her wronged mistress, with the intention of reading it before tearing it into a thousand pieces? Marjory was never able to answer that question, nor could others answer it for her.

She remembered vaguely that she stared at the opening words: 'My beloved and deeply-wronged mistress, what you are about to read is the confession of a dying woman. May Heaven forgive the lifelong deceit that I have practised on you! Lilias is my child, not yours.'

'Ha, ha!' laughed Marjory, at this point, as the blue lightning danced before her eyes. 'O God, am I going mad?' exclaimed the miserable girl. But at that moment, when her brain felt reeling, she saw a small dark object lying on the grass. As she stooped instinctively to pick it up, the sheet of paper she had been reading fluttered from her lap, under the seat; she had torn it across, the fragments still adhered together —but the envelope and the rest of the papers were in her hand.

It proved to be a small book—a worn copy of the Greek Testament. A singular revulsion passed over Marjory as she touched it. That little shabby book was familiar to her. It belonged to Mr. Frere. How often had she seen him read it! It was his constant companion, she knew. In another moment the strangled hysteric convulsion in the throat seemed to leave her; the mad desire to laugh changed into passionate sobs. A flood of tears relieved the tension of the brain. Clasping the shabby little book as though it were a warm human hand, Marjory wept the bitterest tears she had ever shed in her life.

They did their healing work effectually. Her power of thought returned. Her first action, as her sobs subsided, was to restore the papers to their hiding-place in her bosom. She had replaced the envelope, but the torn paper had escaped her recollection.

'Better destroy nothing,' she muttered. 'Who can tell what may happen?'

There was no conflict now, after this outburst of passionate despair. If Marjory's conscience spoke, she refused to listen to it.

'A lie will cost less than murder,' she said

aloud. 'Of the two sins I will choose the least. May God forgive me if it be a sin, but I cannot with my own hands kill Lilias!'

A dull repetition of words seemed to surge in her ears and blend with the storm. She seemed listening to them, and not to the thunder, as she sat still, with the lightning playing harmlessly around her:

'She would try to satisfy them both; but I think any mother's heart would break over such an impossible task. Her own child would appear to her in the light of an interloper.'

And again, in a younger voice:

'If I had been Lena, I should have died. I could not have lived a minute. What! lose my mother!'

And Lilias had heart disease, and was excitable, and she had promised Dr. Ainslie to be careful.

Her thoughts were clearing rapidly now. Her mind was taking a quick bird-flight over past and present and future.

'For Lilias,' she was saying to herself; 'yes, and for my mother, too. Mother—my own mother, I must leave you! Fate is too hard for us. You shall not break your heart over an impossible task for me. If I killed Lilias—and the news would kill her—you would never love me. You would look upon me as worse than an interloper; you would never regard me without a shudder. Better your calm kindness than that; better any loss and misery to myself. The secret is my own. No one but myself has a right to meddle with it. If I choose to lay aside my birthright and go back to my friends, what is that to anyone?'

The hard look of misery in her eyes began to change into a great softness.

'He will be good to me, he will comfort me. I shall be quite safe with him;' and she pressed the little book between her palms. 'I will tell him that I am unhappy, and ask him to take care of me; and perhaps the pain will grow less by-and-by. He must not know the truth for a long time; there will be no need to tell it. Oh, I must go back to him soon! I cannot stay here any longer.'

The thought of her friend was calming her more and more. As the recollection of his tenderness became more vivid, she suddenly started from her seat. The rain was falling in torrents, but the trees had prevented it from wetting her.

What would he say if he saw her sitting, at the peril of her life, in the midst of such a storm, closed round by those dark woods? Had she any right to break his heart as well as her own? What would he and Anne do without their darling torment? At least, she was necessary to them.

As these salutary thoughts returned, Marjory moved quickly though the dell. At any other moment in her life she would have been terrified at the risk she ran. The storm was at its height. The trees crackled and strained under the fierce blast. Torn branches blocked up the narrow path. The zigzag lightning lit up the dim arcades with phosphorescent brilliancy; the artillery of heaven reverberated between the hills.

But as Marjory hurried along she was hardly conscious of the tumult. A single thought had taken possession of her, and seemed to vibrate within her still more loudly.

'For Lilias!'—that was all it said. 'What matters anything that happens to me? Oh no; it is all for Lilias!'

CHAPTER XI.

THE LETTER OVERLOOKED.

MARJORY hoped to gain her room unperceived. In crossing the open lawn to the house the heavy torrents of rain had thoroughly soaked her thin black gown. The gay little handkerchief she had tied over her head was now nothing but a flimsy rag, and her hair was streaming with wet. She tried the door of the conservatory, and found it unlocked; but as she ran up the staircase she encountered her faithful little handmaid, Emma. The girl's rosy face looked quite pale with concern.

'Oh, miss!' she exclaimed, as she caught sight of Marjory's wan, draggled appearance, 'you have given us all such a fright! Mistress has sent Fleming to look for you. We thought you were safe in your own room until a quarter of an hour ago, when they sent me up to tell you Fleming had brought in the coffee. Oh dear! oh dear! do you mean you have been in the wood in this awful storm? I must go down and tell mistress and Miss Lilias; they are so anxious about you.'

'Wait a minute, please,' returned Marjory, in an exhausted voice. 'I think you must help me to get off my wet things first.'

She said this not so much with a view to her own comfort, for she felt strangely careless about that; but in detaining Emma she would put off answering her friends' inquiries.

'Yes, indeed, miss; and if you will take my advice, you will just go to bed, for you are shivering with the dampness and the fright. Why, the water is running from your hair, and your shoes and stockings must be soaking!'

'Very well,' replied Marjory indifferently.

It was easier to carry out Emma's suggestion than to face those two with any pretence of cheerfulness. She let Emma brush out her damp hair and plait it afresh, and heard her praise its luxuriant growth, in a sort of dream:

'For it touches the ground as you sit, miss; and it is as thick as thick can be. Miss Lilias's is nothing to it; and—is it not strange?—it just matches mistress's in colour; and my mother always says that sort of hair is very uncommon. There, you are shivering again! You must just be quick into bed, and I will run down and bring you some hot coffee.'

But it was not Emma who brought the coffee after all. Marjory, who was lying with her eyes fixed on the driving rain, felt a slow shiver creep over her as the low, musical voice she knew so well accosted her.

'Oh, my dear!' exclaimed Mrs. Carr anxiously, 'how you have frightened us! I was so absorbed with Lilias—for you know a storm often makes her hysterical—that I never noticed that you were not following us to the house. What possessed you, my child, to endanger your life by stopping out in the wood?'

'A storm never frightens me, and the rain has only just come on,' returned Marjory.

She spoke in a curious inward voice, as though strength had suddenly failed her; and indeed her senses seemed blunted and numb. As Mrs. Carr offered her the coffee, her hand trembled so much that Mrs. Carr held the cup to her lips.

'You are quite faint, Marjory,' she said tenderly. 'When you have drunk this, you must lie quiet and go to sleep.'

But at her words a frightened look came over the girl's face. How was she to lie there, listening to the rain, and the moaning of the rising wind in the trees, and not go mad?

'Do not leave me!—surely you will not leave me?' she said feebly, as though remonstrating against some act of cruelty, and her hand fastened on Mrs. Carr's gown. It was a soft grey satin, for Mrs. Carr never wore anything but the richest materials. As Marjory's hot fingers seemed to cling to it with a child's persistence, Mrs. Carr kissed her forehead soothingly.

'My dear, of course I will stay with you if you need me; but are you sure that you are not ill, Marjory?—that you have not caught cold? You look feverish, and yet your lips are pale. What would your friend say to such carelessness? I cannot bear to think of your imprudence. Fleming has just told me that the old oak at the foot of Scarsgill has been struck by lightning.'

'The unhappy do not die young,' she replied, with a smile so sad that Mrs. Carr felt touched. 'But I ought not to be selfish,' rousing herself. 'If Lilias wants you, you must go to her.'

'I need not go yet,' returned Mrs. Carr, who had placed herself close to Marjory, and had taken the girl's hand in hers; 'she is reading to Barry now—that will amuse them both. She was a little hysterical when we got back to the house. I think that story upset her, Marjory; it was so sad, I could not get it out of my own head. I am afraid it will haunt me, though I am not generally fanciful. If you are not too tired, dear, I wish you would tell me how it ended.'

Marjory shuddered involuntarily, and turned on her pillow until her face was hidden against Mrs. Carr's shoulder.

'The end was the worst of all,' she whispered, in so low a voice that Mrs. Carr had to stoop over her to hear it. 'When she — the real daughter—knew how things were between those two, and that her mother could not love her, and did not want her, and that the knowledge of the truth would make all their lives miserable, she determined to leave them in ignorance, and go away, though it broke her heart to do it.'

'Oh, how dreadful, Marjory! It does not sound right, somehow. Poor girl, what a martyrdom!'

'She did it for the best,' in the same choked voice.

'It was a mistaken sacrifice, and yet it was a noble one,' mused Mrs. Carr. 'I ought to read the story, and then perhaps I could judge of it better. Please do not let Lilias talk about it any more. I never like her to hear anything sad. Ah, well! this life would be a poor affair if things were not put right in another world. The mother would know her child then, Marjory, and would bless her for the love which, though mistaken, sought to save her pain.'

An inward sob shook the girl's slight frame. Mrs. Carr felt rather than heard it, and put her arm round her.

'Do not talk any more now, darling; I am sure you are not well. Try and sleep, and I will sit beside you as quiet as a mouse.'

Her motherly heart was full of solicitude for this girl, Miriam's daughter, who seemed so unhappy. As she put her arm round her, Marjory seemed to nestle to her as naturally as though she were Lilias. A complete exhaustion, overpowering mind and body, had set in ; the warmth, the coffee, the touch of those motherly arms, seemed to soothe the inward agony. Before long, a profound drowsiness weighed down her eyelids, and in a little while she was asleep.

Mrs. Carr sat patiently beside her in the fading, dim light, until she felt that she might venture to free herself without rousing Marjory; but she had some difficulty in loosing the hold upon her dress. As she stood for a moment beside the bed, an involuntary feeling of admiration seemed to rivet her to the spot. 'She is more than handsome—she is beautiful,' she thought. Marjory's attitude as she lay had the careless abandon and grace of a child ; her face looked pale by contrast with the dark brown plaits that curled about her pillow ; the firm, rounded arms, the beautiful hands — all arrested Mrs. Carr's attention.

'She is too beautful and too aristocratic for Miriam's daughter,' she said to herself. 'How can she have got those finely-formed hands from either Robert or Miriam ? I noticed her foot, too ; it is as small as mine, and has the same arched instep. Lilias has not either a pretty foot or hand. How strange it is! In spite of her paleness, Marjory looks the picture of health, while my poor darling——' But here Mrs. Carr sighed and turned away. She never cared to own, even to herself, how fragile Lilias often looked in her sleep.

Marjory slept profoundly until morning, nor did she wake until Emma stood beside her, with a letter in her hand. Marjory looked at it rather languidly. There was an oppression and weight upon her, but a full consciousness had not returned. By-and-by she would realize her own hopelessness, but just now physical weariness was upon her.

She testified no curiosity about the letter, though Emma held it up before her with rather an important face.

'You left it in the pocket of your black dress, miss, and it has not even been read. It was wet through, so I dried it as well as I could, and I think you will be able to read it. It has the Moorbridge post-mark.'

'Yes, thank you. I must have forgotten it yesterday. You may leave it, Emma.' But she was in no hurry to read it. She drank her tea, and looked out at the grey dreariness of the morning. The window was open, but a heavy morning shower was splashing the creeper and filling the ledges with little pools. 'Another wet day,' Marjory sighed bitterly, and opened her letter.

But before she had read many lines a change came over her face; her eyes grew troubled; her hands shook. In another minute she had sprung up, and commenced dressing herself with feverish haste. 'Would she be in time?' she asked herself almost wildly. Fool that she was, not to have opened that letter yesterday! It was from Anne, and was written very hurriedly.

'MY DARLING CHILD,' Anne wrote,

'I am afraid what I have to tell you will give you pain. It is always hard for me to do that, and especially as the news will reach you on the very day your poor mother is to be buried. But Capel would not let me write before; he said what was the use, when he had made up his mind? You know how peremptory he can be sometimes. And then he never could bear you to be troubled.

'Marjory, darling, Capel is leaving us. He says that he has been idle long enough, and that there is plenty of business for him in Japan. He wants to help his friend settle his affairs. You know how often he has threatened to go; but now he is in earnest. He says it is business and the claims of friendship; but, of course, I know it is all his restlessness, and because some strange trouble has overtaken him.

'But the trouble cannot be helped: my own child, whom I love next in the world to Capel, do not think I am blaming you—never—never! How could such a thought come into my mind? Nothing can come between us two—nothing!

'But all the same I am grieving about Capel. It is hard that my only brother should leave me, and for such a time. He says he will not promise to come home for two years. He has always wanted to write a book about Japan; and he must study the country and the people thoroughly; and he says, over and over again, that we two will be quite comfortable and happy together— as though we shall not miss him every hour of the day.

'It has all been settled in such a hurry that my brain is in a whirl. I wanted to write and ask you to come home, but Capel would not listen to me. He said he hated good-byes, except on paper. They only harassed people's feelings, and did no good; perhaps you may agree with him, Marjory. But I hold a different opinion. I think it is something to grasp a person's hand and bid God bless him, even if it be only a friend who is leaving us—but Capel! Oh no; he is wrong! I am sure you will be unhappy if you do not wish him good-bye. But there is no time now, for the day after you receive this letter—the evening, I mean—indeed it may be quite late in the evening, towards night—Capel goes down to Southampton, for they expect the *Eurydice* will start from the docks the following day. I wanted to go with him and see the vessel, but he will not allow me even to do that. He says he would rather see the last of me in the morning-room at Murrel's End.

'I shall be very lonely when he is gone; but I know you will soon come and cheer me up. Forgive me if I do not write more now, dear.

'Your loving
'ANNE.'

And folded in this letter there was a slip of paper in Mr. Frere's handwriting.

'Do not be sorry about this, my dear child,' it said. 'Remember your sermon to me on the East Hill, when you accused me of wasting my life.

'Well, I have something to do worth doing, so I mean to go over to Japan and do it thoroughly. It is never too late to mend, is it, Marjory? Never too late, I humbly trust, to gather up the "fragments that remain."

'I will write you plenty of long letters by-and-by, when we have once steamed off; but just now I am overwhelmed with business.

'I am leaving you to Anne, a most sacred charge; take care of each other, my two blessings, and be as happy as you can be. Remember I love you so entirely and fully that I desire nothing but your happiness in the completest sense.

'I do not wish to bid you good-bye; it is too painful an ordeal for me. I said it to you in its truest sense on that seat in the wood when I renounced my madness; now I say nothing but God bless you, Marjory!

'Your friend until death and beyond death,
'Capel Frere.'

She had read those words which were never to fade out of her heart and memory again, and then with nervous rapid fingers she had commenced a hasty toilet. Before it was finished she rang her bell.

'Emma,' she said, in a voice the girl hardly recognised, it was so sharp and incisive with pain, 'you have done so much for me, you have been so kind and helpful, that I venture to ask one thing more. In two or three hours I must start for London: will you pack as many of my things as you can? the rest must follow me. Do not question me, please. I have just had news. I have nearly finished dressing. I will tell your mistress myself.' And then she turned away, and coiled up her magnificent plaits of hair with hands that were cold and shaking.

A quarter of an hour later she entered the hall in her brown tweed travelling-dress—her one black gown was hopelessly ruined by the rain.

'Mrs. Carr,' she said, speaking very quickly, and there was not an atom of colour in her face, 'you are so good, I know you will help me. I must go to London by the mid-day train. Emma is packing my things. Will you order the carriage, please, to take me to St. Theobald's? You may read Anne's letter if you will; it will tell you why I must go.'

VOL. III.

Mrs. Carr was not the woman to waste words. She read the letter quickly, and then she said in her quiet way:

'My dear, you shall go if you wish. I would not be so cruel as to keep you. If you had only opened this letter yesterday——' but here she stopped, warned by the troubled look on Marjory's face. 'You shall go if you think it will be any use, but, my child, you see what Miss Frere says—her brother leaves for Southampton to-night.'

'I know,' answered Marjory a little wildly; 'you need not tell me. If I lose hope, if I think there is any chance of my missing him, that he will really go without my seeing him again after all he has done for me——' but here she checked herself, as though afraid of her own agitation. 'God will help me not to be too late,' she finished simply. 'I must ask Him, and leave all that;' and then Mrs. Carr kissed her, and said that she should do as she thought best. She would order the carriage and tell Lilias, and one of the maids should be sent to help Emma.

'And there is no hurry—no hurry at all,' she continued kindly; 'the carriage will not be round for an hour and a half. You must take your breakfast, Marjory, and keep yourself quiet ; for you have a long journey before you.'

Marjory's only answer was to push her plate away, and lean her forehead on her clasped hands. What were food and drink to her ? She did not change her position, as quick footsteps came lightly to her side, until Lilias touched her and made her look up.

'Come, Marjory dear,' she said, in her sweet caressing way; 'mother has told me all about it. We are both so dreadfully sorry. I am going to the station with you. There is nothing I will not do to help you if you will only pluck up courage, and not lose heart. But first, I am going to make you have some breakfast.'

Marjory wanted to say that food would choke her, but Lilias contrived to have her own way. She laid delicate fragments on Marjory's plate, and coaxed and caressed her as though she were a child ; and for very love and gratitude Marjory submitted. In spite of herself, something like hope crept into her chilled heart. She might not be too late, after all. No, she said to herself; God would be too merciful. She had suffered so much ; she would surely not be called upon to endure any further misery.

She looked up and smiled at Lilias as this thought crossed her. It was a poor, pitiful attempt at a smile, and made Lilias's eyes misty. And then she said she would go to Barry. She would not wait until the last minute to bid him good-bye.

Mrs. Carr had prepared him, and he looked at her a little wistfully as she entered.

'I am so sorry you are going, Marjory,' he said, as she sat down beside him. 'You have been so awfully good to me, that I shall miss you dreadfully. You must come and see us soon again. In another month I am to take to crutches, you know, and you and I will have some walks together.'

'I hope so,' she answered gently. 'You must not forget me, Barry, and our long talks, and the books we have read. I shall think of you so much.'

'And I of you,' answered the poor lad, wondering a little at her tenderness. He had never understood her sisterly patience and forbearance, and had often marvelled at it.

Marjory sat quietly for a few minutes, trying to repress the sudden yearning to take the thin hand and cover it with kisses—her brother's, whom she dared not claim.

'Good-bye!' she said at last, starting up as though she found her position intolerable. 'God bless you, Barry! That is better than good-bye, is it not?' And she turned away so quickly that he could not see the tears in her eyes.

An hour after that she was standing at the door, and Mrs. Carr was holding her hand and looking at her anxiously.

'You will not telegraph to Miss Frere to meet you in London, Marjory? I think it would be better.'

'No,' returned the girl decidedly; 'I dare not. He might go away all the quicker, because he does not wish to bid me good-bye, and then Anne would be deprived of her last evening with him. Do not be anxious about me. I know all about the trains. There is one to Moorbridge at half-past eight, and I shall catch it. Please give my messages to Mr. Wentworth and Margaret.'

'Yes, dear child; I will not forget.'

'And,' went on Marjory, looking in the beautiful face so near hers, 'there is much

—much I want to say, but I have no words. Think of me—love me a little——'

And then her courage failed her. She threw her arms round Mrs. Carr's neck, and for one passionate minute those strong young arms held her fast, as though they would never let her go. Then, with a sob that nearly broke her heart, she sprang away; and when Lilias followed her into the carriage, she found Marjory cowering on the cushions, with her face hidden in her hands.

'Dear Marjory, mother is kissing her hand to you, and there is Barry by the window.'

Marjory shook her head. She dared not show them her pale face streaming with tears. She was leaving her rightful home, the mother and brother whom she loved—perhaps for ever. The iron had entered too deeply into her soul for her to look up.

Lilias, with great tact and delicacy, left her to her own thoughts during the long drive. Now and then her hand stole into Marjory's, or a mute caress testified her sympathy. It was not until they had reached the station, and Marjory and she were standing together on the platform, that Marjory opened her lips.

'You will write to me very often, Lilias?'

'Yes, dear.'

'And you will tell me all the Mavisbank news, and when the wedding is to be?'

'Yes,' she answered again, blushing a little; 'I will tell you everything.'

'Oh, there is the train! We had not long to wait after all. Good-bye, Sissie darling! You had better kiss me now.'

They kissed each other a little sadly and solemnly, and there were tears in Lilias's eyes. As Marjory took her seat in an empty compartment, she looked out of the window. Lilias was standing alone on the platform; her grey gown was blowing a little about her feet, and her fair hair was gleaming like pale gold in the windy light.

'Good-bye, Marjory,' she said. 'Do not lose hope, my darling.'

The words seemed to float after her as they moved away from the platform; the sweet face, with its speaking smile, seemed to follow Marjory for many a mile.

'Do not lose hope, my darling.'

And then the wind seemed to die away, and there was the drip, drip of the rain against the window-panes. But for a little while Marjory's thoughts were confused, and she could do nothing but gaze out at the misty hills and flying stone walls, with a feeling of utter blankness that would by-and-by wake into the activity of pain.

CHAPTER XII.

HOPE DEFERRED.

IT seemed to Marjory as though her journey had lasted for days when she at length arrived at King's Cross, and stood for a moment, half-dazed, looking at the wet London pavements, and the watery sunshine that seemed breaking behind the houses. The train for Moorbridge was not due at Charing Cross for a full hour and a half; nevertheless she called a cab, and had herself driven to the station; and putting her luggage into the charge of a porter, went in search of a cup of coffee, and then seated herself wearily in a corner of the large waiting-room, watching the strange faces that passed and repassed in a sort of vacant dream.

Marjory felt as though she had exhausted her

emotions—as though she were capable of no further effort. But it was only the collapse of fatigue, and want of food; the coffee soon revived her, and the old feverish excitement returned.

'If she should be too late!' that was her one thought. Even the agony of her leave-taking, and the knowledge that she was driven forth an exile from her home, and from her mother's heart, faded beside the longing—the almost unendurable longing—to see her friend again. Marjory never asked herself what this craving meant: she only knew that in losing Mr. Frere she would lose everything; that he was necessary to her; that she could not and would not do without him; that her love for Anne was small and puny beside her reverence and affection for him.

But not even to herself would she speak of this; she did not even question herself as to what she should say to him when they met. 'When the time comes I shall know what to say,' she thought; 'but one thing I know, that I shall pray him not to leave me—never to leave me again.'

After this her thoughts became confused: all

sorts of misty recollections seemed to surge into her mind. Now she was on the beach at Whitecliffe, with Mr. Frere beside her; she could hear the waves splashing to her feet in the darkness, and could see the red glow of his cigar as he rambled on in his whimsical way, mingling philosophy and sentiment, while she laughed at him in girlish fashion.

Then she was sitting with Mrs. Chard in the little parlour, in the bright firelight; outside there were the lighted windows of the Crown, the illuminated clock-tower, the tall gaunt masts of the boats, and the dark sea-line. She could hear Lilias singing—no, it was Hurrell, 'All is vanity, vanity;' and there was the knocking of his hammer, and the twittering of the birds in the wood. 'For Lilias,' some one seemed to be saying; 'For Lilias—for Lilias.'

It was just as they were steaming into King's Cross, and Marjory had fallen into a brief doze, lulled by the monotonous motion. For a little while she felt weary and inert, almost numbed into forgetfulness. But as her strength revived, her restlessness returned in twofold force; her corner in the waiting-room became unbearable, and she rose up a little giddily, and began to pace the platform. Another half-hour to wait before the Moorbridge train started.

Many people looked after her, as she walked to and fro with swift uneven footsteps. The tall pale girl, with the sad abstracted face, attracted a good deal of attention; there was something so graceful and commanding in her carriage, that even in a crowd she would have been noticed. But Marjory was quite unaware of the interest she excited—her dark eyes were looking out straight before her, the careworn handsome young face never changed its expression. 'If she should be too late!' this was all she said to herself, over and over again; and sometimes Lilias's voice seemed to answer her out of the summer stillness, 'Do not lose hope, my darling.'

There was a sudden quickening of her pulses as the train for Moorbridge came slowly to the platform. As she took her place she felt that now her journey would soon be over. She even hailed the fast-falling dusk that began to hide the well-known landscape from her, for it told her the longest day she had ever passed would soon have an end. And yet this last hour seemed harder to bear than the rest—her restlessness became positive pain. She was alone in the compartment, and could walk up and down the narrow passage when she could no longer sit still; this was her only relief. She would stand for a moment, looking out at the rising moon, and the dim summer sky, and the flying hedgerows, and then resume her walk again.

Moorbridge at last—for one brief minute Marjory's eyes scanned the platform, but no familiar face greeted her. Then she bade the porter call a fly, and waited impatiently until her luggage was placed on it. 'Drive as fast as you can to Murrel's End, on Woodleigh Down!' she said quickly; but there was something in her voice that made the men look at her.

Poor Marjory! that drive, short as it was, tested her patience severely. The long steep hill that led to the Down could not be climbed very speedily by the poor jaded horse. Marjory shut her eyes, and prayed that she might not be too late; and then opened them, and saw the moonlight shining behind the limes and on the red pantiles. And then the white shutters of Murrel's End came in view; but as the driver was turning in at the gate, she stopped him.

'I do not wish to startle them,' she said.

'I will walk up to the house, and you may follow me very slowly.'

But as she passed into the shrubbery, and saw the lighted window of the morning-room, her courage and strength seemed to fail her, and her limbs trembled with excitement.

The front door was ajar, but she felt no surprise. It was often so when Mr. Frere was taking his evening prowl in the garden. It struck her as a good omen, and a smile came to her face. True, she could hear no voices; but perhaps he was in the greenhouse, or pacing the gravel paths behind the house. She stole into the hall softly, and then tapped at the door of the morning-room.

Anne's voice said 'Come in!' and Marjory stood on the threshold.

But the next moment she told herself that she had known all along how it would be. She knew it without a word, as Fluff rushed to her feet with a joyous bark; and Anne rose from her chair with a terrified exclamation on her lips.

'I am too late, then? He is gone!' Marjory could scarcely frame the words—her tongue seemed so heavy and dry.

Her look frightened Anne, for she burst into tears as she took her in her arms.

'My dear! why have you come? I wanted you, but not like this. Oh, you poor child!' reaching up to kiss her, for she was such a little woman.

'He has gone, then?' repeated Marjory, in a dull voice; but she let Anne draw her to the easy-chair, and sat down mechanically, only her eyes did not leave Anne's face.

'Yes, he has gone!' replied Anne, hardly able to answer for her tears, they flowed so rapidly at the sight of her child. 'You must have passed him on the road, Marjory. He left by the 8.58 train that reaches Charing Cross at half-past ten. There is a train that leaves Waterloo at a quarter-past eleven. He expects to arrive at Southampton about half-past one.'

'And I must have passed him on the road?' in the same inward tone.

'Yes, dear—yes,' fondling the hand she held. 'But you must not take it to heart, Marjory; he could not bear to say good-bye. Capel is so tender-hearted. He would not let me go with him. Oh no, he said; it would make him miserable. He said very little; only he left his love for you, and I was to ask you to come home soon, that you might cheer me up.'

'And you let him go?'

'Oh, my dear!' in a broken-hearted voice; 'how was I to help it?—and he looking so thin and unhappy, and saying he could not rest; and walking all day, and then coming home in the evening, worn out with fatigue, and yet not able to sleep. It is better for him to go, Marjory, bad as it is to part with him. It is better than to see him eating out his heart with restlessness.'

Marjory seemed to concentrate her thoughts with difficulty. She looked long and fixedly at Anne, as though she were trying to read her thoughts. Her forehead was contracted with an anxious frown, but in reality she was laying her plans.

Anne was trembling like a leaf. The sudden shock of seeing Marjory had broken down her enforced calm. She had had a choking feeling of misery all the evening, but had been unable to shed a tear until she saw the girl's despairing eyes. Anne's beautiful little face had grown thinner and paler, and there were grey threads in the bright brown hair; but the tears were a relief, and the sight of Marjory seemed to ease the aching sense of loss.

'Darling,' she said softly, 'I know all about it; and it was better for him to go!'

'He shall not go!' replied Marjory hoarsely. 'Anne, do not cry so—I cannot bear it! Where is the railway guide?—quick, quick!—bring it to me!'

And Anne, wondering, and very much frightened by this sudden vehemence, did what she was bidden to do.

Marjory turned over the pages with feverish haste until she had found what she wanted.

'Look here, Anne; listen to me. Never mind the noise outside; it is only my luggage, and Mackay can see to that. It is past ten now—nearly half-past—and there is no train at all until seven a.m.'

'No train? What do you mean, Marjory?'

'I mean that we must follow him to Southampton—you and I. He shall not go without bidding me good-bye. He shall not. I will not let him. Look here; the first morning train leaves Moorbridge at seven. We must tell my flyman to come for us at half-past six.

The Southampton train starts from Waterloo at nine, and arrives at 11.20.'

'But, Marjory, we might lose the train.'

'We shall just do it; I am sure we shall just do it. If we lose that train, there is nothing before 10.15, and that does not arrive at Southampton until after one. He is to sail at midday, is he not?'

'No; he may go on board, but they will not get off until evening. But, Marjory, my dear child, do give up this foolish scheme. Capel will not like to see us; he may be displeased at our following him. Anyhow, he will be embarrassed and ill at ease, and it is too late to alter his arrangements now. You look so ill, Marjory, you quite frighten me; and you have been travelling all day.'

'Very well, then, I will go alone,' returned Marjory, in the same harsh, strained voice; and without waiting for Anne to answer, she went out into the hall and paid the flyman, and gave him her orders.

'You must not be later than half-past six,' Anne heard her say; 'that train is very punctual.'

And then she went back into the room,

taking no notice of Anne, and began to lay aside her hat and jacket in an absent, mechanical way.

Anne watched her until she could bear it no longer.

'Oh, Marjory!' she said piteously, 'do not be so unkind to me in the first hour of your return! Why will you not speak to me or look at me? Do you think for one moment that I should let you go alone?'

'I do not want you to displease him,' returned Marjory, with forced composure. 'He is your brother, and you ought to know best what will give him pleasure. I will not take you against your will. I will go alone. I am not afraid of what he will say to me.'

'But I shall go with you, all the same,' she replied, in a hurt voice. 'Do you think I should consider my own feelings, when you are so unhappy, Marjory. Oh, my dear, what makes you misunderstand me so to-night? We will go, both of us, and perhaps Capel will not be displeased.'

'He will not; I am sure of that,' whispered Marjory; and then she put her arms round Anne, and hid her face in her neck. 'Forgive me, Anne. I did not mean to be unkind; but if you knew how I have suffered!'

And then she told her how the letter had lain in her pocket unread, and how it had almost broken her heart to know that he was going away without giving her the opportunity of speaking one word to him.

Anne listened in silence. What could she say to the poor child to comfort her? In a few hours Capel would be far away from them both, and they would have to bear their loneliness. Perhaps, if Marjory had her wish, and could bid him good-bye, she would be more reasonable and happy. Anne, in her simplicity, never guessed at what was passing in Marjory's heart. Her pure, reticent nature forbade any curious prying into the girl's mind. She believed Marjory's love for Capel was altogether filial, and imagined that in a few weeks his absence would cease to trouble her.

Marjory was grateful for this silence. It was a relief to pour out some of her overcharged feelings. She was so sure of Anne's sympathy, so certain that no troublesome questions would be asked her.

They talked together for a little while, hand-in-hand; and then Anne insisted that a proper meal should be prepared for her, and went in search of Mackay. Marjory offered no objection. She knew that ministry and loving service were the strongest instincts of Anne's nature. To wait upon those she loved was her highest form of happiness.

The dull pain faded out of Marjory's eyes as she watched the small womanly figure moving busily to and fro, the busy hands occupied in her service. She ate and drank obediently, as Anne bade her; only when her friend tried to persuade her to go to bed for a few hours, she turned suddenly restive.

'I have been resting all day,' she said plaintively, 'and I should not be able to sleep. A warm bath and a fresh change of clothes will refresh me, and then I will lie down. I might get a nap then.'

And Anne wisely forbore to press the point.

But going into her room an hour later, she found Marjory ready equipped for her journey, and sitting by the bedside with heavy eyes and cheeks pale from her midnight vigil.

'Now, you must lie down, my dear,' she said in her gentle way, 'and I will lie beside you;

and Mackay will call us in time for our early breakfast.'

And she took the tired girl in her arms as though she had been a child, and, to her delight, soon heard the light, regular breathing that told her Marjory had fallen asleep.

'Thank God!' she thought; 'she will not wake now until Mackay calls us;' and she was right. Marjory slumbered peacefully, and woke in the summer sunshine with Anne's voice in her ear:

'There is no hurry,' she said, as Marjory started up in vague alarm. 'The fly will not be round for half an hour. Bathe your face in cold water. Mackay is making us some coffee. I am so glad and thankful you have slept, my child.'

But Anne never added that she had not closed her eyes, and that her head was throbbing ominously.

Marjory was very silent as they drove to the station. How fresh and beautiful everything looked at that early hour! The birds were singing loudly; the dew sparkled on the yellow gorse of the common; the air felt fresh and sweet, blowing from the uplands.

In spite of herself, a little hope crept into Marjory's heart. She would not be too late again. Oh no; that was not possible. How could she despair, with God's blessed sunshine lying round her, and all the sweet sights and sounds of nature?

It was not until they were in the train and were miles away from Moorbridge, that she noticed Anne's paleness and jaded looks.

'Oh, Anne, you have one of your bad headaches coming on!' she exclaimed in dismay; for here was a fresh difficulty.

'Never mind,' returned Anne faintly. 'I could not sleep, that was all. You must take the lead, Marjory, for these headaches make me so stupid. If I close my eyes and do not talk, it may pass off in an hour or two. The name of the hotel is the Waverley. You will not forget that;' and she tried to smile as she spoke.

But her excessive paleness frightened Marjory. She knew what these headaches meant. They always followed any violent emotion or fatigue, and kept Anne prostrate for hours.

Marjory watched her, sorely troubled, until they reached Waterloo, and then there was not much time to lose. Marjory drew Anne's arm through hers, and hurried her along the platform.

'We shall just do it!' she exclaimed breathlessly, as Anne sank back on a seat, half-stupefied by a sudden accession of pain. 'Oh, how cruel I am to you!' she went on remorsefully. 'I have made your head worse, dragging you along so quickly; but now we are in the Southampton train you will have nothing to do but to rest.'

Anne made no answer; she was trying to hide from Marjory how ill she really felt.

'I said we should just do it!' cried the girl hysterically, as the guard put them into the compartment and immediately gave the signal for departure. Marjory added, 'Thank God!' to herself, as she darkened the windows, out of pity to Anne's aching eyes, and tried to make her comfortable. Happily she had some eau de Cologne with her, and she could wet her handkerchief and lay it on Anne's forehead. It was only this that kept her from fainting; but she bore her sufferings as usual without complaining, and tried to cheer Marjory by telling her that she would be better soon.

The journey was miserable enough to them both. Anne fretted inwardly because she had failed Marjory just when she needed her most; and Marjory blamed herself for selfishness. She should have come alone, or taken Mackay. Anne was not fit for the journey, and she ought to have known it.

There was no help for it now; she must do the best for Anne that lay in her power. As soon as they reached Southampton, she called a cab, and desired the man to drive them as quickly as possible to the Waverley Hotel; it was not far from the station. As soon as they stopped, Marjory left Anne for a moment, and went into the hotel to make inquiries.

The waiter asked her very civilly to wait a moment while he went in search of the landlady. In two or three minutes he returned with a pleasant, comely-looking woman.

'Yes; Mr. Frere was in the hotel. He had arrived about two that morning, and had had his supper, and had gone to bed. He was still in his room—number twenty-four—and had ordered breakfast to be laid in a private room. He had just rung for his hot water— Charles was going to take it. Was there any message the young lady would like to send up to him?'

Marjory reflected for a moment, and then said, 'No; she only wanted the number of his sitting-room, and she would join him by-and-by; but she had a lady with her who was suffering from a severe headache, and she must ask the landlady to show them at once to a bedroom.' And then she went back to Anne.

'We are not too late. He is here; he is not out of his room yet,' she said quickly, as she went back to the cab.

Anne gave her a little smile, and pressed her hand; and then she let Marjory support her into the hotel.

'Do not stay with me; this young woman will do all I want,' she said, as the chambermaid came to them to volunteer her services.

But Marjory refused to listen to this; she must see to her first, she said quietly, as she took off her hat and jacket and prepared to wait on her.

The room felt close, so she opened the two windows; then she bathed Anne's face and hands, and laid wet cloths upon her forehead. Anne submitted gratefully for a little while; then she took hold of the busy hands.

'Dear Marjory, I shall lie here quite comfortably; I do not feel faint now, only the pain will have its way for a few hours. Tell the chambermaid to come in now and then and look at me, but she must not ask me questions; and now go down to Capel, and make his breakfast for him.'

'I am going,' returned Marjory, in a low voice, 'but he is not down yet; his room is next to this, and I can hear him moving about. How little he guesses who are his next-door neighbours!' and she laughed nervously.

That going down to meet him was not quite so easy as she thought it would be last night. Her excitement had ebbed, and she felt a little dismayed at her own temerity.

'I wish I did not look quite such a scarecrow,' she said mentally, as she smoothed her hair; 'but it cannot be helped.' And then she went slowly downstairs, casting furtive glances behind her, and went in search of the sitting-room, which she found without much difficulty.

It was a snug, shady little parlour, looking out into a quiet street. The two windows were open; there was a stand of scarlet geraniums with some mignonette in one of them—the room was sweet with it. For ever after the scent of mignonette brought back the memory of that morning to Marjory.

The breakfast-table was laid, and the *Times* lay beside the plate. Marjory walked round the room, looking at the pictures; then she took up her position by the window, and tried to interest herself in the passers-by.

There was a flower-seller, with a white puny baby in her arms; the woman was marked with the small-pox, and had a weak, hopeless-looking face. 'How unhappy she is, and what a sickly baby!' thought Marjory; and she called her to the window, and threw her a shilling.

'You may give me as many flowers as you like,' she said indifferently, 'but I like roses best.'

She was quite surprised at the size of the bunch that was handed to her; but she took the flowers so carelessly that they fell on the window-seat, and it took her some time to arrange them. A little crimson rosebud, just opened, attracted her attention, and she laid it on the *Times*. How often he had gathered flowers for her—and this bud was so young and pretty! Just then the opening door startled her so, that the flowers fell from her hands again. It was only the waiter, however, with the coffee-pot and a covered dish, and Marjory turned again to the window.

There were some church bells chiming—for a wedding, most likely; and then some grey pigeons flew down from the portico, and began strutting about in the dust; a wiry terrier came out and barked at them, and a little ragged boy, with a monkey and a hurdy-gurdy, limped slowly down the pavement. He saw Marjory, and began to tune up after the manner of his kind, and the monkey hopped feebly on to his shoulder. Marjory shook her head at him, and threw him sixpence; and the boy trudged away, grinning from ear to ear.

The dreary grinding of the doleful instrument had prevented Marjory from hearing again the sound of the opening door.

'Oh, what a world it is!' she said aloud; 'nothing but hungry women and children in it, pain and sorrow everywhere.'

'Good God, it *is* Marjory!' exclaimed a voice behind her; and as she turned herself quickly, Mr. Frere came up to the window, and stood beside her.

CHAPTER XIII.

'YOU KNEW ME BETTER!'

'WHEN the time comes I shall know what to say;' that was what Marjory had told herself confidently over and over again: yet no sooner had the familiar voice sounded in her ear, no sooner had she looked up and seen the shrewd, kindly face, and the keen eyes that seemed searching her through and through, than a great confusion and timidity kept her tongue tied; and though she turned her head aside quickly, he could see that her cheeks, and even her lips, were white.

But, even in that swift upward glance of hers, she had noticed that a great change had passed over him. He looked graver, thinner, as though some shock or illness had befallen him—as a man might look who had tasted of some great bitterness, and had taken a long leave of hope. All this was written legibly in his face; and yet there was a dawning wonder, and something of the eagerness of an unexpected joy in his eyes.

'Marjory, it is you! and yet I thought I must have been dreaming!'

'Yes,' she said in a low voice, but not looking at him. 'Anne and I have just arrived.'

'Anne here?' in still greater astonishment.

'Yes,' she repeated; and now the colour began to ebb back into her face, perhaps because she was conscious how he watched her. 'I made her come; she was very hard to persuade at first, because she said you would be displeased. But no; I told her that I knew you better than she did.'

'You knew me better than Anne did,' he repeated slowly; and there was a strange meaning and doubt in his voice.

But it escaped her, and she went on more rapidly:

'Anne is ill. She could not sleep last night, and she has one of her dreadful headaches. She is lying down upstairs in the room next yours, and the chambermaid is looking after her. I was to come down and make your breakfast,' she said; 'and that reminds me, Mr. Frere, that your coffee is getting cold.'

'Never mind!' detaining her as she was about to move away from him. 'Marjory, tell me one thing. Have you come all this way just to bid me good-bye?'

'I wanted to see you again,' she returned, with downcast eyes. 'It was cruel of you, cruel, to go away and leave me without a word. I would not have believed it of you.' And here her voice trembled. 'I told Anne that I would not bear it—that I could not help it whether you were displeased with me or not.'

'Marjory, you are giving me something very precious to carry away with me. My heart will not be quite so heavy to-night.'

She flashed a sudden appealing look at him; and he could feel her fingers fluttering in his grasp in a helpless frightened way. Go—he would go after all! And how was she to stop him? How was she to speak the words that alone would keep him by her side? A sort of despair fell on her. Surely he might understand her without any words.

'Come,' he said gently; 'you are too pale,

Marjory Doo. I have driven the colour twice out of your face already. You used not to be so afraid of me. There will be plenty of time to talk by-and-by, for I do not go on board until evening. Sit down, dear, and we will breakfast together, and you shall pour out my coffee, just as you used to do at Murrel's End. See, I will ring for another cup and plate; and if the omelette be spoilt, that is your fault, and not mine.'

'I have had one breakfast already,' she said, with a little laugh. 'It was rather an early one, however; but still I am not hungry.'

But she might as well have talked to the wind. Mr. Frere insisted on summoning the waiter and giving him very particular orders. There was to be fresh coffee made, and some cream brought. The young lady liked cream, and the omelette was a failure; but there might be cold ham—yes—and a pigeon-pie. Oh, he thought a pigeon-pie would be a capital *pièce de résistance*.

In vain Marjory protested that she could not and would not eat.

Mr. Frere insisted that the table should be covered with provisions. Marjory was helped liberally, and then he made a pretence of setting her a good example. The pie, he said, was excellent, and so was the coffee; but though he said this, there was very little food taken by either of them: for how could he eat in that sweet young presence, when the girl's eyes were dim with trouble, and there was that childish quiver on her lips? He laid down his knife and fork presently, as though the task were beyond him.

'Did you come all the way from St. Kilda's to bid me good-bye?' he said at last; but his eyes were on his plate as he spoke.

'Yes,' she returned, somewhat reluctantly. 'By some accident, I forgot Anne's letter with your note inside, and never opened it until yesterday. I made up my mind then that I would come at once; that after all those years you were treating me cruelly in leaving me without a word, and that I would not bear it.'

'I did not mean to be cruel,' he said, defending himself. 'Men do not feel like women in this; they cannot endure piling up agony. There is the parting. Well, that is pain enough, without saying good-bye. It is better to get it over without a word—when the word almost chokes a man to speak it.'

'I do not feel like that,' she answered. 'I would bid my friend God-speed—if he would go—but——'

'But what, Marjory?'

But she would not finish her sentence.

'By-the-bye,' he went on lightly, 'Anne was afraid of displeasing me by coming, was she not? But you knew better than that.'

'Oh yes,' she returned, falling at once into the trap laid for her. 'I told Anne that I knew you better than she did.'

'Well, that is strange!' in a musing voice; 'and yet Anne and I have lived together all our lives. But you knew me better than she did, Marjory! How long have you gained that knowledge, dear?'

She looked up at him, startled for a moment; but, in spite of the vagueness of his words, there was no mistaking his expression. She knew then that she was understood. She put up her hands to try and hide the flush that suffused her face. Then her head went down on them lower and lower. She would rather have died than have said a word.

He waited silently for a minute or two.
Perhaps he found it difficult to speak too.
Then he quietly raised her face and looked at it,
and a low murmur of satisfaction that was almost
a blessing escaped him.

'Is it so?' he said. 'Is such a miracle
possible? And I am not to go after all, Marjory?'

'No,' she whispered, and now her face was
hidden on his shoulder. 'You are never to
leave me—never to leave me again.'

'You know what you are saying, dear?'
touching her hair caressingly. 'You know that
I can only stay as your husband—not your
friend.'

He understood her, with some little difficulty,
to say that was what she meant, but it was not
for her to say it.

'I will try to believe it,' he said presently,
when they had been silent for a little while, but
the wondering look was still in his eyes. 'If
I ask you every hour of the day if it be true,
Marjory, you must bear with me, for I think I
am almost dazed with this unexpected happiness.
This morning I woke the most miserable wretch
in the world, thinking years would pass before

I should have the courage to see your face again. I opened the door, expecting vacancy, and there you stood in the sunshine, with this rare gift in your hand. Are you sure—are you quite sure—that you really mean it—that my grey hair does not frighten you?'

'It does not frighten me at all,' she returned shyly.

'Come and let us sit down,' drawing her to the low couch that stood between the windows. 'It wants the strength of youth to support such a weight of happiness; and there is so much that we have to talk about, and there is no need for us to stand. I do not feel that I can understand things properly. Do you remember, dear, that day in the Mavis Woods, and how you bade me hope nothing? "Do not hope—do not—do not!" that was what you kept saying.'

'Yes, I know;' and the tears came to her eyes. 'I could not help saying that, you took me so much by surprise. I think,' in the lowest possible voice, for she was still very shy with him, 'that I began to repent directly you went; but I never knew what I really felt until I read that note, bidding me good-bye.'

'No,' he repeated, and there was a strange

brightness in his eyes. 'And you really feel that you can love me well enough to marry me?'

'I think so—I hope so,' she faltered; and she said a little piteously: 'I do not love you now as well as I ought; but if you will be patient with me, I am sure that it will soon be all right. Your loving me makes me happy, and I never want you to leave me again.'

'That is enough to satisfy me,' he replied, soothing her, for she was becoming agitated at his questions; and then he went on telling her very gently that he was sure now that she cared for him, even when she refused him, though they neither of them knew it at the time. That she must never blame herself for the pain she gave him then, for her sweetness and honesty on that occasion had made her far dearer to him; that though she was so young, only one-and-twenty next month, and he was nearly a quarter of a century older than she, that he was not afraid to let her engage herself to him, or to marry her. 'For you must know, my sweet,' he finished, 'that a conscientious man will never marry a woman unless he feels that he is the one person likely to make her happy; and I feel that I and no other man should be your husband.'

They talked a little longer, until she was calm and happy again; and he had made her laugh by telling her that Mr. Frere was a tabooed person, and that he never meant to answer to any name but Capel.

'But it seems taking such a liberty,' she objected, with a blush.

'You will find that it is a liberty quite to my taste,' he answered, smiling; 'and though it may be difficult at first, I am not quite such a Methuselah that I am to be debarred from the use of a Christian name.'

And when she found he was a little sensitive on the subject, and that her refusal would hurt him, she promised to do her best to get used to it.

'Now that weighty matter is settled, there is something else that I must do,' he observed, starting up from the couch. 'Do you know that you have upset all my arrangements, that my passage-money is lost, and that my luggage may be on board for all I know? I must leave you for some time, Marjory; there is the captain to see, and the steward, and all sorts of business to settle; then there is Anne to be considered. You will never get her back to Moorbridge to-night.'

'I never thought of that,' returned Marjory, and her face clouded a little. 'And yet how are we to stay?—we have brought nothing with us.'

He considered this question gravely—bringing all his man's wit to bear upon the difficulty. Then he said gravely that he would go in search of the landlady, and see what she could recommend on the emergency; but when he returned a quarter of an hour later, his whole air was jubilant.

'We have ordered such a dinner, Marjory! I never knew such a sensible woman; her ideas are tremendous. She said of course the ladies would like champagne, and they had a first-rate brand; and I said yes, of course, because I could see she expected it. Then as to your little difficulty, why, she was full of resources; she will find everything for your use and Anne's— putting it all down in the bill. She has daughters; I saw one of them—a pretty girl about your height; and if there was anything that you wanted to buy—well, her daughter could get it; there are plenty of shops in Southampton. By-the-bye, I must do a little business myself this afternoon'—and here he looked mischievous. 'You never wear rings, Marjory—oh, I have noticed that—but I think I shall know your size; and—my dear, you are surely not going to leave me?'

'I must go to Anne; she has been left long enough alone,' returned Marjory, making her escape. 'Good-bye until evening, Mr. Frere. Oh, I forgot—but I will do better next time,' laughing at him from the doorway.

Anne was looking very white and wistful, as Marjory entered; her head was really better, she said, and the maid was fetching her some strong coffee.

'If I lie quiet for two or three hours, I shall be able to come down; but, Marjory, why does not Capel come and see me?'

'He thought he had better not,' she answered, keeping her face well out of Anne's view; 'he does not sail to-night after all, Anne. You will see him to-morrow and the next day.'

She did not dare to say more than this in Anne's weak, suffering condition. When her head was really better, she would tell her all; but she dared not bring on a return of the pain. As it was, tears of relief came to Anne's eyes.

'I shall see him to-morrow; and why not to-night, Marjory?'

'He is going out now—he has so much business to settle. If you are better, you can come downstairs, and partake of the grand dinner he has ordered. Do you know, he has been extravagant, and has actually ordered champagne.'

Anne smiled faintly.

'I mean to come down. I am sure the pain will not last much longer. Oh, I am so thankful that we have come, and that he is not vexed with us! Did he seem at all vexed, Marjory?'

'He was astonished, and very much pleased; it has quite cheered him up,' replied Marjory, going as near the truth as she dared. 'We had breakfast together, and he ordered up a great ham and a pigeon-pie, and neither of us ate anything. I think the waiter will laugh when he sees our plates; and he told him to bring cream, because I was so fond of it, and I quite forgot it. He will think us funny people, will he not, Anne?'

'And what did you and Capel talk about?'

'Oh, we talked about — things,' returned Marjory desperately. 'But here comes your coffee, Anne. Do you know'—yawning a little

—'I am getting very sleepy again. We had such a broken night, and all that travelling and anxiety has taken it out of me.'

Marjory was only speaking the truth. Her excitement was over; and the intense relief—the knowledge that her friend would never leave her again—made rest possible. She felt a strange weariness, a delicious languor creeping over her; and at Anne's suggestion she drew an easy-chair to the bedside, and, laying her head against the pillow, soon sank into a dreamless sleep.

Anne lay and watched her. She thought Marjory's face looked a little thin and worn in her sleep; there were lines round the mouth she had never noticed before.

'She has grown older in the last few months,' she thought. 'Now her poor mother is dead, one great source of bitterness will be removed from her life. No one can claim her now—she is my child and Capel's.' But Anne never dreamt of the secret that lay in Marjory's breast, and how a living mother was asserting natural rights over the girl's affection.

A slight movement in the room at last roused Marjory. Anne was standing by her.

'My dear, you have had such a nice long sleep, and I think I must have dozed to keep you company, for the pain has quite left me. Capel has been in his room—I heard him moving about. It is past five, Marjory, and you say he has ordered dinner at six.'

The mention of Capel's name banished Marjory's drowsiness at once.

'Oh, I must go down to him,' she said hastily. 'He will wonder what has become of me.' And then she blushed a little at her own words, and turned away to smooth her hair.

'Tell him that my headache has quite gone, and that I will be down soon,' observed Anne innocently; and Marjory nodded assent.

She was anxious to evade Anne's scrutiny, but when she was outside the parlour-door a sort of shyness at the thought of seeing him made her hesitate a moment. She could hear him pacing restlessly up and down the room, as though he were marvelling at her absence. As she turned the handle he came up to her at once, and there was impatience in his voice.

'Where have you been, Marjory? I have

been hurrying back to you, and you have kept me waiting all this time. You must have known how I should be longing to see you again.'

He spoke reproachfully, but there was a great softness in his eyes as he looked at her.

'I was asleep,' she answered simply. 'You forget how tired I was.'

'I think I forget everything but what you told me this morning. Look here, dear! see what I have brought you. No; give me your hand first. It will look better in its proper place.'

And in another moment a magnificent half-hoop of diamonds was blazing on one of Marjory's slender little fingers.

'Is that for me?' she asked, with almost awe in her voice. 'Oh, it is far too beautiful, Mr. Frere!—Capel, I mean.'

'Thank you,' he said, kissing her. 'That was brave of you, dear. Hush! Here comes Anne!'

And, with almost boyish embarrassment, he released her, and went to welcome his sister.

'You are looking pale, Anne, my dear,' he

said, leading her to a chair; 'but you will soon get better now.'

'Oh, I hope so!' misunderstanding his meaning. 'Capel, I was thankful to hear that you were not vexed at us for following you.'

'Oh no!' he returned, laughing a little nervously; 'I was not vexed at all. Far from it.'

'And you have two days more to spend with us?'

'Two days!' looking at her in a bewildered sort of way. 'Do you mean that Marjory has not told you?'

'She has told me nothing but that;' and, to her surprise, Capel turned suddenly very red.

'Why,' he stammered, 'I have made up my mind to stay quietly at home.'

He broke down here, and Marjory tried hard to keep from laughing; he was so evidently out of countenance, and it was impossible to go to his relief. And there was Anne, looking from one to the other in a painfully anxious manner.

And how they would have got out of the

difficulty neither of them knew; only just then Anne caught sight of the diamonds, and, by a sort of feminine inspiration, guessed the whole truth.

'Oh!' she gasped, and there was a low, sobbing sigh of relief, and she turned very pale; but before either of them could speak, she had taken her brother's hand and kissed it.

'Capel—dear brother, is it true? Marjory, come to me! You have made me so happy! Darling, to think you came to us out of the snow for this!'

And then she could say no more—only cried softly to herself from sheer happiness; and Marjory cried a little too, out of sympathy.

Mr. Frere said afterwards that he was just going to take up his hat and fly, but for the opportune appearance of the waiter. The sight of a fellow-man restored his courage, and fortified him with the prospect of dinner. It was a privilege, he said, to watch that man. His folding of napkins was an art; and he thought his sister and Marjory would have done better to take lessons from such an artiste, than to sit whispering together hand-in-hand.

He rallied them on this subject between the

courses—indeed, he kept up such a flow of conversation, perfectly unaided by the two women, that the waiter, in spite of his stolidity, was evidently impressed by his eloquence; and when that functionary had withdrawn, he declared that he was wound up to that pitch that nothing short of a speech would relieve him, and he called upon Marjory to witness that he had only twice filled his glass with champagne.

He delivered it in his usual fashion, walking up and down, while Anne and Marjory sat by the open window.

He began by self-laudation. He said he was surprised himself—in fact, overwhelmed with astonishment, to see what a successful thing he had made of his life, and he could only account for it by his extreme love of philosophy and his great patience in waiting. Young men generally made a mistake at the beginning. They were like Impatience in the 'Pilgrim's Progress.' They wanted all their good things at once, and they got through them as rapidly as possible. At thirty they had exhausted everything; they were *blasé*; and they agreed with Solomon that there was nothing new under the sun.

He was thankful to say—indeed, he was

modestly elated to know—that he was not one of these young men. He had taken life quietly, diluting his pleasures so that they lasted longer. Domestic life had been to his taste, and he had enjoyed a good spell of domesticity. He had had his little experiences. Well, perhaps they had been painful at the time; but, like a burnt child, he had evaded the fire ever afterwards. He had travelled, he had seen the world, he had enjoyed the sweets of bachelorhood and club-life. Many were the pipes he had smoked, and a total absence of responsibility had made him sleep sweetly at nights. He knew many henpecked husbands and careworn fathers of families who had considered him an enviable person. He quite agreed with them. But the grandest point of all in his career had been that he had trained and educated his future wife most carefully, that——

Here there was a little scornful protest on Marjory's part, at which he quietly smiled, but went on in the same fluent manner:

To some people her youth might have been an obstacle, but it was none in his eyes. Proud as he was of his grey hairs, he was prouder still to think that he had embued her with his philosophy and indoctrinated her with his own peculiar views. As a matter of course, he did not think much of women's rights. He considered they talked a great deal of rubbish; but he was thankful to know that the young person who had consented to be Mrs. Frere was perfectly docile and submissive, and never advocated her own opinions. And then, as Marjory's eyes flashed at this audacious speech, he suddenly broke off and came up to her.

'It is a lovely evening. Will you go out with me, Marjory?' he whispered very gently.

But it was not with this sort of talk that he beguiled her as they walked together in the sunset, until the stars came out and peeped at Marjory leaning on the arm of her grey-haired lover, as they stood together by Southampton Water.

CHAPTER XIV.

UNEXPECTED TIDINGS.

THE next day they returned to Murrel's End, and took up the old life again—the old life, and yet how changed to Marjory!

But for the knowledge of her secret, and the sad yearning pain that filled her whenever the thought of Mavisbank and its inmates recurred to her, she would have been perfectly happy. Every day she was drawing closer to her future husband—every day she was learning more of his noble, unselfish nature. As her reverence deepened, her love increased; and very soon she could echo Anne's words—that there was not a man living to equal Capel.

She felt herself to be what she really was—

the light of his eyes, and the hidden treasure of his heart. Now there was no further need of reticence; he could pour out, without rebuke, the whole wealth of his love on her. Marjory almost trembled as she listened; she was so conscious of her own faults, so aware that she never even aimed at the standard he allotted her. But when she hinted at this, he told her gravely that she was not faultless to him, that she never had been, but that he loved her so well that he hardly noticed her defects.

The only cloud between them lay in her unfortunate secret. Marjory could not always hide her sadness from him. Once or twice, even in the first weeks of their engagement, he had come upon her unexpectedly, and had found her trying to banish hastily the traces of tears for which she could give no reason.

Once he sat down beside her, and reasoned with her gently.

'Marjory,' he said, 'you are very nearly perfect in my eyes, but there is one flaw in your character—you are not quite generous. You are giving me yourself, but not your whole confidence.'

She murmured something—that it was not

always possible to give that; but he shook his head at this fallacy.

'My dear,' he said, 'Anne and I have taken great pains with your education, but in one branch you are showing yourself a decided dunce. Do you know there ought to be no reservations between husband and wife, or between engaged people? You are wearing my ring, and we are already thinking of fixing the day, and yet you are still keeping that secret from me.'

Marjory looked up at him with wide-open frightened eyes:

'What secret do you mean, Capel?'

'The one that has made you unhappy ever since you went to Whitecliffe. Do you remember your words?—you spoke them on this very bench: "One day I will come to you of my own accord." Has not the time come, Marjory?'

'No,' she whispered; 'and you promised me then that you would not ask me again.'

He sighed restlessly.

'Well, but I thought things were different with us now. You had not promised to marry me then. Think how I am circumstanced, and take pity upon me! I love you more than anyone in the world, but when I see you unhappy I am not to ask the reason.'

This touched her, as he knew it would.

'Dear Capel, I am quite happy when I am with you. If there were no one to consider but myself, I would tell you now. But I dare not! I dare not for the sake of others.'

'Do you mean that this secret does not concern yourself, but only other people?'

'It concerns more than myself,' she answered ambiguously. 'My telling it might lead to infinite trouble.'

'Why so?' with the keen glance she dreaded. 'Do you think I should not guard your confidence most sacredly—as you would mine? Have I not a right, as your future husband, to know all that concerns you?'

'You have the right,' she answered, dropping her eyes, 'but you will be generous, Capel, and not claim it. You will trust me a little longer?'

'I suppose I must,' he returned reluctantly; 'but I do not feel easy, Marjory. You are so young, you have so little knowledge of the world—evil-minded people might dupe you very easily.'

'Yes; but I will never do anything again without asking your advice,' she replied coaxingly.

'Will you promise me that?' turning on her quickly. 'Will you promise me faithfully, Marjory, that as soon as possible you will tell me this thing; and that until then you will never take a single step without coming to me first; and that if any fresh difficulty, any new complication arises—I am talking in the dark, you see—you will then be perfectly open with me?'

'Yes,' she replied very soberly; 'I think I can promise you that.'

'And, Marjory,' here his voice became very persuasive, 'will you not think very seriously of what I said last night? We have been engaged a month—it is nearly the end of August now. To-morrow you will be one-and-twenty, and you will be Nellie Walford's bridesmaid. Nellie is setting you an excellent example, and there is every inducement for you to follow it. Your friends at Mavisbank have inundated you with congratulations; they, as well as Anne, heartily commend your taste. Now, my dear, you remember that I am not a young man, and that in my case there is nothing to warrant delay. I see Anne is judiciously acting on my hints, and, as we have agreed that any sort of fuss would be obnoxious, the sooner we settle this business the better.'

Marjory listened with a heightened colour, but her answer was not ready. He had spoken to her more than once on this subject, and she had felt the force of his reasoning. No, he was not a young man; and, as he had told her, there had been very little joy in his life. His early manhood had been clouded by disappointment, and he had passed many years in aimless, desultory wanderings. 'I have done very little good in my generation,' he had said sadly, 'though I have harmed no one. Child, do you remember your little sermon on the East Hill? The arrow shot at a venture most certainly pierced my armour—there.'

And then he had gone on speaking, but very gently, so as not to alarm her. She was very young, he said, but that was a fault that time would cure; and no one could say that he was not old enough to take care of her. He congratulated himself that he had sufficient knowledge of the world for them both. He almost rejoiced that his hair was grey when he remembered this.

'So, my dear,' he had concluded, 'as we have known each other intimately for eighteen years, we have nothing more to learn about each other's character. You were always a reasonable creature, Marjory, and I am sure your good sense will plead for me. And,' he continued, in a wily manner, ' you will find Anne is quite of my opinion.'

All this had been said to her on the previous day; and in the evening, when they had been alone together, Anne had spoken on the same subject, dropping little hints that showed in what groove her thoughts ran.

It was about Nellie Walford, so soon to be Nellie Brooks, that she had been talking; but she branched off a little from that topic, and asked Marjory if she did not think long engagements very wearying to both parties; but as Marjory held no particular views on this matter, she had gone on—rather hesitatingly—to give her own opinion.

She thought — yes, she certainly thought that long engagements were to be deprecated— they unsettled young people dreadfully; and when, for example, the gentleman was not very young——'

'Ah, I know what you mean!' interrupted Marjory, with a blush. 'Dear Anne, you need not beat about the bush. Capel has been worrying me about that already. I tell him that I am in no hurry; but that does not seem to make any difference. I never knew he could be so masterful.'

Anne smiled. She thought it possible that Marjory knew very little about men, and how they could employ the craft of the serpent, and the innocence of the dove, to compass their own ends. She took the girl's glowing face between her hands and kissed it.

'Marjory, I hope, for Capel's sake, that you will not be adverse to an early marriage. It is a little hard for a man of his age to act the lover—not but what he can play that *rôle* more perfectly than even younger men; but I think he would be happier if he were settled. He has told me so, and I believe him. He shall not hurry you too much, dear; but when next he speaks to you, I hope you will fix some date that is not too distant.'

Marjory was pondering over Anne's words,

as she sat by silently listening to Mr. Frere's arguments. The idea of an early marriage was not distasteful to her; she would lay aside that odious name, then. No one would ever call her Miss Deane again. If it were only for this reason, she was quite willing to marry him as soon as possible. And never once did the thought cross her of the risk she ran by marrying under a false name.

But she had her own ideas on the subject, and when he had finished what he was saying, she replied a little irrelevantly:

'Capel, do you know—oh, I forgot I never told you—I had a letter from Lilias, yesterday. Such a dear letter; and she says they are afraid that their marriage will have to be put off until the spring, because of poor Mrs. Wentworth. She is very ill—dangerously ill, they think.'

'I am sorry for that,' he returned gravely. 'Wentworth has waited too long already; that sort of thing tells on a man.'

'Yes, I am sorry for him,' observed Marjory softly; 'but Lilias will be quite happy to wait.'

'You can be sorry for him, and not for me,' pretending to frown.

'Oh, I have not kept you waiting long,' she replied lightly. 'I will promise to be reasonable, but then you must be reasonable too. Listen to me, Capel: most people do not like winter weddings; but for me, I do not mind them at all. New Year's Day—now I think that would be a grand day—the best day in the whole year to begin a new life.'

'Four whole months to wait,' he returned, in a grumbling voice.

But he was well pleased, for all that; he had feared his bird would have wanted a longer flight than that.

'They will soon pass,' she replied quietly; 'and nothing would induce me to be married this year.' And here the strained restless look came into her eyes. 'We will begin the new year together, if you will.'

'Yes, yes,' he returned eagerly; but he wondered a little at the pain in her voice.

'And, Capel,' in a still more agitated manner, 'promise me that it shall be very quiet. I could not have a wedding like Nellie's—oh, not for worlds! Lilias says she means to be my bridesmaid, as I cannot be hers; but I will have no bridesmaids—oh, none at all! I want you and Anne to take me away to some quiet place, where no one will notice us, and we can go to church together just as though there were no marriage.'

'Why, Marjory!' he exclaimed in surprise.

But when he saw the beautiful dark eyes were full of tears, he repressed his astonishment, and only tried to comfort her.

'Nothing could suit me better,' he returned cheerfully. 'I will tell you what we will do, darling. We will go down to Whitecliffe in December—you and Anne can go to some nice lodgings, and I will put up at the Crown—and I will come and fetch you for long walks; and we will go to the East Hill and to the Castle, and to all our old haunts. And in the evening, when I have finished my dinner, I will tap on the window, and you will come out to me, and we will walk up and down the parade in the darkness. And then, when New Year's Day comes—well, what can be easier? We can drive to the little church, you remember; and in half an hour the whole thing will be accomplished.'

'Oh, I am so glad you do not object,' she replied, clasping his arm gratefully. 'You are doing it to please me, I know; but indeed you have lifted a weight from my mind.'

'That is well,' he returned, still more cheerfully. 'Now we must go back, or Anne will be wondering what has become of us. Look at those clouds, Marjory. It has been very sultry all day—I expect we shall have a storm before night.'

'Oh, I hope not. Ever since that evening in the Mavis Woods I have hated storms;' but here she checked herself in alarm.

'Were you out in a storm, then?' he asked, looking at her.

'Yes, and I was alone. Oh, it was horrible!' and she shivered and hurried on; the remembrance was a sort of nightmare to her.

'Perhaps it will pass off,' he replied soothingly, as he watched her.

It was this kind of change in her that troubled him. They would be talking happily together, and Marjory would be laughing; and all at once, at a word—some chance word—she would turn pale, and a strange look would come into her eyes, and she would sink into silence.

'If I could only find out what troubles her,'

he would say to himself; 'when she is my wife, I shall know then. I shall find a way to make her speak—I am sure of that.'

They were both a little silent, as they entered Murrel's End. Mackay met them at the hall-door. Her mistress was out, she said: she had been called down to Lupin Cottage, as old Hawthorne was much worse; and they were not to wait dinner, in case she should be delayed.

'Very well,' observed Marjory; and she would have passed on, only Mackay detained her.

'There is a telegram and a letter for you, Miss Marjory, in the morning-room. The boy had a deal to say about the telegram. There was a mistake in the address; it has been to Groombridge, and Uxbridge, and I don't know how many -bridges. But it seems you ought to have got it the first thing this morning. Mistress was in a hurry, or she would have opened it.'

'I have never had a telegram before!' exclaimed Marjory. 'I hope—oh, I hope there is nothing wrong!'

'Nonsense!' replied Mr. Frere, laughing at her. 'Why, I have received hundreds of telegrams, and not one has told me bad news.

You are nervous, dear. Shall I open this wonderful telegram for you?'

'Yes, please,' she returned, in a frightened whisper. And still laughing at her, he tore the envelope open.

'Why, it is from Margaret Ainslie,' he began; but, as he glanced at the message, a shocked look came over his face, and he tried to cover the paper with his hand.

'My dear, this is dreadful,' he said in a grieved voice; but she would not let him go on, only tore the paper out of his hand.

And this was what they both read:

'Lilias is dead—she died quite suddenly. I will write full particulars. Barry wishes it.'

CHAPTER XV.

'IT WAS A TERRIBLE MISTAKE!'

'LILIAS is dead!'
'Was it true? Could it be true?' that was what Marjory's eyes seemed to ask him, for she could not speak. How could she, when the words seemed frozen on her lips?'

'Dear,' he said, very gently—for he understood that voiceless question—'I fear it is true; there can be no mistake about it. This is a sad shock for you; but we must see what Miss Ainslie says in her letter.' And as he put it into her hands, a look of anguish crossed her face.

'I cannot read it, I cannot. Oh!' with a choking sob, 'it was for Lilias I did it—only for Lilias. And now it has all been in vain.

Capel, it will kill my mother—her life is bound up with Lilias.'

'Dear Marjory,' he said, wondering at this—for her words were inexplicable to him—'your poor mother is at rest; no sorrow can touch her now. Neither must we grieve too sorely for that bright spirit that has taken its flight. She always seemed to me as innocent as a little child, Marjory. And we are told that "of such is the kingdom of heaven."'

'I know it,' she returned. And now the tears were running down her face. 'She was too sweet and good for this world. But it is of my mother I am thinking—my dear, beautiful mother—who will be breaking her heart alone.'

'What do you mean?' he asked, sorely perplexed—for he could make nothing of this. 'Is it of Mrs. Carr you are speaking—of Lilias's mother?'

'No,' she returned, between her sobs; 'it is Lilias's mother who is dead, but mine is living. Oh no, I am not wandering; it is the truth, and you must believe it. It was for Lilias I came away; and now she is dead, and my mother thinks she has no daughter at all.'

Mr. Frere had grown almost as pale as

Marjory in his great surprise. No, she was not wandering; there was some method in her madness. In that second there flashed into his mind a conviction that she was speaking the truth. That wonderful likeness to Mrs. Carr, that strange unlikeness to poor Miriam. Good heavens! was this the secret she had been keeping from him? Was it possible that she had had the strength to endure all this alone? What was it she had done? What did those words mean? Had she discovered her rightful inheritance only to renounce it—for Lilias's sake? Oh, it was incredible, impossible! There was much that he must ask, but not now, when she was almost convulsed with those passionate sobs. She must be calmer before he could speak to her. He put his arm round her and drew her to a seat, and then he fetched her some water, and made her drink it.

'Now you are a little better,' he said, placing himself beside her, 'and you will like me to read you the letter, that we may see how things are. I will read it very slowly, and you will try to follow it, will you not?' And though she did not answer, he could see that she checked her sobs to listen.

'"Dear Marjory,'" it began, '"I have promised Barry to tell you everything. He says that you will be so sorry for them, and that you loved her so; but indeed, everyone loved her. I found afterwards that I had sent the telegram too late, and that the office was closed, and so you will get my letter a few hours after it has arrived. I know you will be dreadfully grieved, Marjory; but my father tells me that the news will not be so great a shock to you as to others, as you knew that our dear Lilias had heart disease, and that her life was a precarious one. He says he had tried to warn her mother, but she had refused to understand his hints.

'" But now I must tell you all from the beginning, and if my hand shakes, you must forgive that, for the tears will come into my eyes as I write.

'"How I wish you could see her now! I think you would feel less sorrowful. She looks like some beautiful angel, or a child who has fallen asleep with a smile on her lips. We see the purity and the innocence so clearly stamped on her dear face. Do you remember what her mother once said of her—" that she was only fit for a world where there was no marrying or giving in marriage"? you repeated that speech to me. Well, I think it was true; she was one of God's little ones, and He has called her home, because she was young and weak.

'"But, now for my sad story:

'"I had gone up to Mavisbank that afternoon, because they had found fault with me for being such a stranger; and as I had some few hours at my disposal, I thought I would surprise them with a visit.

'"I found Mrs. Carr alone in Cosy Nook. She said Lilias was not feeling very well, and had complained of the heat; and she had gone to her favourite seat in the wood. I might join her if I liked; and Hurrell was coming presently, and she should send him after us.

'"I was very willing to go, for I was longing for a talk with Lilias. I knew my way to the dell perfectly, and I was not long in reaching it.

'"I never shall forget how lovely it looked. I never heard the birds sing as they did that afternoon, as I stepped across the grass. I thought Lilias was asleep. Her hat was lying on the bench, and the sun shone on her hair; one arm was leaning over the back of the seat, and her face was half hidden on it. It was just the attitude of a child who had grown weary of play, and had fallen asleep.

' "I remember I smiled as I stooped over and kissed her; and then I wondered that her face was cold, and that she did not move; the next moment a terrible fear seized me. Surely she looked very strange! I took hold of her, and called her loudly; and then all at once I understood what it meant. Marjory, I knelt down for a moment, and asked God to give me strength to carry the dreadful news; and then, without giving myself time for thought, I ran through the wood. But before I could reach the house I met Hurrell.

' "He was whistling in his old merry fashion; but, when he saw my face, he stopped and stared at me.

' "I hardly know what I said to him; he asked me if anything were the matter, and I answered, 'Yes; something very dreadful had happened, and he must be prepared for a great shock.' And he said, still staring at me in a fixed sort of way, 'Has it anything to do with Lilias?' and I gave a great sob, for the words would not come, and pointed up the path.

'"'You must speak out!' he said, gripping my arm quite angrily; 'where is Lilias? what has happened to her?'

'"His face frightened me, and I remember I begged him to be calm for her mother's sake—it would kill her mother. I said she was on the bench in the wood, and he would see for himself; for somehow, I could not tell him she was dead. But, when he had heard me so far, he flung my arm away, and tore down the path, and I followed him as quickly as I could.

'"But before I could get to the dell I could hear his footsteps returning; he had her in his arms, and he called to me quite fiercely to let him pass.

'"'She has fainted,' he said in a hoarse voice—'you were wrong to leave her; but her mother will know what remedies to propose!' And though I called after him—though I begged and implored him not to let Mrs. Carr see him—though I prayed him that I might go first, and prepare her—he was perfectly deaf to my voice. He had laid her on the couch, and her head was on her mother's lap; and that was how I found them.

'"He would not believe that she was dead;

nothing would make him believe it. My father came and spoke to him—there was nothing to be done, he said : life had been extinct some time. And he turned on my father, when he said this, as though he would have struck him. I do not know what we should have done, only Mrs. Carr came up to him as he stood there almost raving—poor Hurrell!—and drew his head down to her shoulder, and called him her poor boy—her dear son, and begged him in a heart-broken voice not to add to her trouble, for their darling was in heaven. And then she could say no more ; but was it not beautiful of her, Marjory, to try and comfort him ?

'" He is a little quieter now, and I never leave them—my father says that I must not ; and, indeed, I am too thankful to be here.

'" Poor Barry frets sorely ; he thinks more of his mother than himself. If she could only cry, but the tears will not come—and I fear she does not sleep. She spends hours looking at Lilias, and sometimes I see her smile ; I think she is following her to Paradise, then. I like to hear her say, 'How happy she looks, Margaret!' for I know she has forgotten herself then. Dear Marjory, I think I have told you everything. Barry sends his love, and says you must come to them by-and-by.

     ' " Yours lovingly and sorrowfully,
      ' " MARGARET." '

'My dear,' he said very quietly, when he had finished, ' this is a beautiful letter that Margaret has written. I am glad these poor souls have so faithful a friend to minister to them in their trouble. Now you must listen to me, dear child! I want you to lie down on that couch and try to compose yourself. I shall leave you alone a little, that you may gain strength to talk to me by-and-by, for there is a long story that you have to tell me, and you cannot speak to me now. " The righteous are taken away from the evil to come;" try to remember that, and you will mourn less bitterly for your friend. No one shall disturb you; when Anne comes in I will tell her all that is necessary;' and then, looking at her very kindly, he closed the door, and left her alone in the evening sunshine.

 It was good of him to leave her; she felt that for a little while she could do nothing but weep. She remembered how solemnly she and Lilias had kissed each other on the platform that miserable morning. How Lilias had stood there with the wind blowing her grey gown about her feet, and a smile on her sweet face. 'Do not lose hope, my darling!' that was what she said. And as the vivid recollection came to Marjory, she thanked God in her heart that she had spared Lilias that terrible pain. 'I am glad of it now, Sissie,' she said, speaking half aloud; 'if it were all to come over again, I would not do otherwise.'

Presently the door opened noiselessly, and Anne entered, bearing a little tray; there were tears in her kind eyes as she set it down and kissed Marjory.

'Capel says if you love him, you will take what he has sent you; it will give you strength for the talk you are to have together. I am not to speak to you, Marjory; he will not have you disturbed. But I must say one word, dearest—God knows best: we must believe that, even when His hand lies heavy upon us.'

'Yes,' whispered Marjory, pressing her cheek for a moment against Anne's; and then, as Mr. Frere's will was law to her, she ate and drank obediently.

And she felt, as all of us must feel, that food

given by loving hands in the first hours of a bitter grief is a sort of sacrament—strengthening not only the body, but the soul, and refreshing it. Half an hour later, when Mr. Frere came back to her, he found Marjory seated by the open window, waiting for him. She held out both her hands to him, and said in an unsteady voice :

'I am quite ready to tell you all you wish to know; it will be an untold relief to get rid of this terrible secret. But there is something you must read first;' and she put Mrs. Chard's confession into his hands.

He took it from her gravely, and began to read. But before he had turned the first page, his hand sought hers, and held it firmly; and then, without a word, he went on to the end.

'Now you must go back to the beginning, and tell me all that happened to you at Whitecliffe,' he said, in the same quiet dispassionate voice; and she obeyed him as submissively as a little child.

Perhaps he guessed the relief that it would be to her to pour out without stint or reserve the whole of that bitter story; for he never interrupted her by a single question—only an encouraging pressure of the hand he still held so closely spoke of his absorbing interest.

But, indeed, no question was needed. Marjory told it all, without omitting a single point: Lilias's accident; Mrs. Chard's self-betrayal; the long miserable scene that had passed between them; Mrs. Carr's arrival; and Marjory's yearning affection for her true mother.

She told him of her life at St. Kilda's—her love for Barry—her feverish nights and restless days; the anguish she endured at witnessing that perfect love that subsisted between her mother and Lilias; the calm kindness to the young guest that fretted her so sorely, and kept her at a distance; her growing hopelessness of results as Lilias's fragile health and sensitive temperament became apparent to her.

Then she narrated to him the account of Mrs. Chard's death, and Lilias's sweet pity for her old nurse. But when she came to the evening of the storm, and those terrible hours during which she was making up her mind to become an exile for Lilias's sake, her voice broke, and she could hardly finish for the sobbing breaths that hindered her utterance.

If she could only have seen the love and pity in the eyes that never left her face—strong man as he was, he could hardly suppress his emotion as he listened. What generous folly had this girl wrought! what madness of heroism—what reckless self-sacrifice had she contemplated that would have wrecked them all, and brought them to utter confusion!

'Marjory,' he said, when she had finished, 'all is clear between us now. The last shadow has fled. Thank you, my darling, for telling me all. It was generous, it was dear of you to act as you did; but, my child, it was the most terrible mistake you ever made. If you had only come to me and told me all! Marjory, I tremble to think of what might have happened but for the news we have received to-day.'

'What do you mean?' she asked in a frightened tone, for he spoke with a gravity that was almost solemn.

'My child,' he said, caressing her, 'what did I tell you? That you were so young and ignorant of the world. Well, was I not right in saying this? We are engaged, and on New Year's Day we are to be married. And you would have been married under a false name—and Lilias also!'

'Oh, Capel!' hiding her face in her hands, as the meaning of his words crossed her mind for the first time. But with all his gentleness and pity for her, he would not spare her; she must realize the danger she had escaped.

'We were to be married by banns,' he went on quietly, 'and Lilias Marjory Carr would have been married under the name of Marjory Lilias Deane, and the marriage would not have been legal; and Lilias too—well, there would have been the same mistake, and what a complication that would have been!'

'Oh, Capel! please do not say any more. I never thought—I never dreamt of that.'

'Why, no,' he returned slowly; 'I suppose not;' but he was smiling now. 'A man would not have committed such an error, unless he did it purposely, out of sheer wickedness, and wished to render his engagement null and void. Only a silly enthusiastic girl could have been guilty of such a piece of madness.'

'You are hard on me,' she whispered, without lifting her face; it was burning now.

'I do not mean to be that,' he said, with

great gentleness. 'I am afraid it has made me love you all the more. I only want to show you where you have erred. You were trying to act the part of Providence—to decide on your own destiny and the destiny of others. Marjory, what does the Bible tell us? "We may not do evil that good may come." It would have been surely an evil to act a lie all your life.'

'I did it for the best,' she said very piteously.

'I know it,' he returned, with some emotion. 'You listened to your generous foolish heart, and never heard the prompting of the inner voice, "This is the way, walk ye in it—the way of truth, of perfect upright dealing, of doing unto others as we would they should do unto us."'

'Oh!' she said, bursting into tears at this, 'you are disappointed in me. You will never think the same of me again.'

His only answer was to take her in his arms, and soothe her as though she were a little child who had wandered out of the path. He said a few words to her by-and-by that completely satisfied her and removed her rankling doubts for ever.

'Capel,' she said presently, 'you will take me to my mother, will you not?'

'I have thought of that,' he returned. 'Dear, of course you shall go, and I will take you. Do you think I shall trust you by yourself again?'

'And we will go to-morrow?'

'No, not to-morrow, or the next day. We have your mother to consider, Marjory. Leave her alone in peace with her dead. Margaret will be with her. She will not want sympathy. Let Lilias be laid in her grave first, and then we will go. It will be a shock to your mother, you must remember that. She may not be fit to bear it.'

Marjory was a little sorrowful at this decision, but he would not listen to another word. Anne would be wondering at this long conversation, he said, and he thought it was time that she should be enlightened. Marjory was too weary to bear any more, and he begged her, in a voice that admitted of no appeal, to leave him with his sister and to go to her own room.

'Anne shall come and wish you good-night,' he finished. And Marjory was thankful that his kindness shielded her from the trial of repeating it all to Anne.

But it was late, and Marjory was sinking into a doze before Anne came to her bedside. If her room had not been dark with the summer twilight she would have seen how pale Anne's face was, and how red her eyes were with weeping.

Her voice faltered a little as she bade her good-night.

'You will try to sleep, Marjory dear? I am thankful, for your sake, that your mother is living. I am quite ready to give up my child!' she brought out the words bravely, but a little huskiness betrayed her.

'Anne, you have been crying!' putting her arms round her neck. 'Do you think that finding my mother will make any difference between us? Shall I be less your child because I am hers? Never, never! How can you accuse me of such ingratitude, when you took me, a miserable little child, out of the snow that Christmas Eve, into the warmth of your heart and home! It will be Mizpah always with us, Anne;' and the gentle creature listened to the girlish voice that pleaded with her so lovingly, and was comforted.

CHAPTER XVI.

'WILL YOU FORGIVE YOUR MOTHER?'

NE bright September afternoon, Marjory and Mr. Frere were walking up the long, ugly street of St. Kilda. They had passed the night at York, where they had left Anne to admire the grand old Minster at her leisure; and there she meant quietly to await their return.

No one but Margaret knew of their expected arrival, and she had begged them to call at her father's house before they went on to Mavisbank. A note from her lay at that moment in Mr. Frere's pocket.

'There is something I must tell you,' it said. 'Will you contrive to be alone with me for a few minutes? I have asked my father to detain Marjory on some excuse. I told him there was a little business that you and I had to settle together.'

It was these few words that were making Mr. Frere secretly anxious; but his cheerfulness returned the moment Marjory spoke to him.

'There is Margaret,' she exclaimed, 'watching for us!' And her steps quickened a little, and the next moment Margaret came out and welcomed them.

She was dressed in mourning, and her grand face looked thinner and paler than it used to look; but the lovely, short-sighted eyes had their old tranquil expression.

'Dear Marjory,' she said, embracing her, 'this is a trying ordeal for you. It was good of you to write and tell me the truth; you knew it would be sacred to me, and that I should keep it even from my father.'

'Mr. Frere wished me to write,' returned Marjory, with downcast eyes. 'He said we might need your help, and that he knew you were to be trusted.'

She gave him one of her sweet smiles, and then she turned again to Marjory.

'Your mother is better; we hope she is better. She cried a great deal yesterday, and that has been a relief; and we think she slept last night. Barry is so good to her—he hardly ever leaves her. It was seeing him come in on his crutches for the first time that broke her down. She said how happy it would have made Lilias, and then she was hysterical. Oh, Marjory, her patience and submission are something wonderful —they teach us all a lesson.'

'There is Dr. Ainslie, Marjory,' observed Mr. Frere at this moment. 'You know you wanted to speak to him. Will you not join him in the garden?'

'Oh yes!' she returned, drying her eyes, and quite oblivious of the significant look that passed between him and Margaret, as he followed her into the parlour.

'Well,' he observed, as soon as they were alone, and Margaret had carefully closed the door, 'I hope you have nothing to tell me that Marjory may not know.'

'That is for you to decide,' she returned, in a trembling voice. 'Mr. Frere, no one knows of this but myself—no one will ever know, if you should will silence. This is what I took out of Lilias's dead hand that afternoon in the wood.'

He looked at her with a sort of dread in his

eyes as he took the paper from her. It was torn across and was much soiled, but the writing was perfectly legible. It was Miriam Chard's handwriting—he knew that at once.

'My beloved and deeply-wronged mistress,' it said, 'what you are about to read is the confession of a dying woman. May Heaven forgive the lifelong deceit that I have practised on you! Lilias is my child, not yours; she is my own daughter, and Robert Deane—not Philip Carr—was her father——' And here the fragment broke off.

'Good heavens!' he exclaimed; and then he looked at Margaret, and a paleness crossed his face. 'It was Marjory who dropped that,' he said; 'she told me she tore it in atoms, not knowing what she did; and Lilias found it, and — O my God!—it must have killed her!'

'Yes, but she had heart disease,' she replied soothingly. 'My father tells me now that she might have died any night in her sleep. Marjory must never know this—you would not wish it?'

'No, no!' with a shudder. 'Give it to me; I will destroy it. You have acted wisely, Miss

Ainslie: I owe you deep gratitude for this!' And he held out his hand to her.

She had died, that happy creature, of a broken heart. The shock that Marjory would so generously have spared her had been too great for the feeble frame to bear. The sun was shining, the birds were singing round her as she read her death-warrant; one moment's incredulous agony —one shuddering sigh—and then the merciful angel we call Death drew near and took her in his arms to rest.

At this moment they heard Marjory's footsteps in the passage, and Mr. Frere turned to the window a moment to recover himself; but Margaret met her with a smile on her face, and talked to her in a low voice. In a few minutes he joined them.

'We must go now, Marjory. Miss Ainslie, you have promised to follow us: do not be long; we may be in need of your friendly help, if our task prove difficult.'

'It will be difficult,' she answered. 'I have told Marjory so, and I have begged her to be very careful. At first it will be a shock; the pleasure and the comfort will come later.'

'You are right,' he returned gravely; and

then he took Marjory's hand and placed it on his arm. She was very brave, very patient; but he knew what she was feeling. 'Dear,' he said very tenderly, as the gates of Mavisbank came in view, and he felt her hand tremble, 'you will try to control yourself, for your poor mother's sake, will you not?'

'I will try,' she answered, but her lips were very pale; and then they walked up the garden in silence.

The door stood wide open; the afternoon sunshine was streaming through the old hall, lighting up every nook and corner, and falling full on the solitary figure seated beside the desolate hearth.

For one moment Marjory caught Mr. Frere's arm, as though her courage failed her.

Mrs. Carr did not turn her head; the sound of their footsteps had not reached her. She was sitting in her high-backed chair, with her back to the window; and in her deep mourning, and stately immobility, she looked like some bereaved queen. Her hands lay folded together in her lap, and her beautiful features looked as though they were chiselled in marble, they were so fixed and impassive.

'Hush, dear! we must not startle her,' whispered Mr. Frere anxiously; and he would have detained the girl, but she broke away from him with a choking sigh.

'Do not look so,' she cried, holding out her hands most piteously; 'it breaks my heart to see you sitting there alone! Dear mother, darling mother, I have come to comfort you; Capel has brought me.'

The word 'mother' seemed to rouse her, and she looked from one to the other with a sort of dull surprise. There was a faint trembling—a convulsive movement—in the throat, and she said in a toneless far-off voice:

'Is that you, Marjory? This is kind of you, my dear, to come and see me in my trouble—and Mr. Frere, too. I wish Margaret were here, that she could welcome you properly. I am very weak, and not quite myself, and I do not understand what I ought to say to people.'

'Dear mother,' returned Marjory, kissing her hands passionately, 'there is no need for you to talk to us. It is enough for me to be with you and wait on you.'

Mrs. Carr raised her eyes to Mr. Frere, as he stood beside her. They had a dim faded look, like the eyes of a person who had not slept.

'Why does she call me that? Tell her not to call me that; it hurts me, for I have no daughter now. No, that was wrong,' speaking in the same gentle mechanical way. 'I have my child still, though I cannot see her sweet face. But she calls me mother sometimes. I can hear her voice plainly as I sit here in the evening. "Mother, my own mother!" oh, quite plainly I hear it!'

'Dear Mrs. Carr,' he returned, and there was something in his voice that held her attention, 'will you try and listen to me a moment? You have lost one child—yes, it is true, her bright young life is ended in this world—but God is very merciful, and you have still a daughter living; and Marjory is that daughter.'

She shook her head mournfully, as though she failed to understand him. She thought, poor woman! that they were trying to comfort her by offering her the loving service of the girl who was still clasping her hands.

'No one can take her place; that is empty for ever,' she replied.

'Can you bear a great shock?' was his answer

to this. 'Can you forgive a dead woman's miserable scheming and lifelong deceit? Mrs. Carr, you trusted Miriam Chard with your child, but she betrayed your confidence. It was your child, not hers, that she lost. It was her child that you took to your heart, and brought up as your own daughter. Your adopted daughter lies in her grave; your own child, Lilias Marjory, is holding your hand now.'

He had spoken with slow, quiet emphasis, that every word should sink into her brain. He had motioned Marjory to be silent, and had spoken himself. But for a moment he was terrified at the result of his words. Her eyes had not left his face, but as he went on a grey veil seemed to creep over her features. As he stopped, she fell back in her chair, as though she were fainting, only her eyes remained wide open. It was with intense relief that he heard Margaret's footsteps on the gravel; Mrs. Carr seemed to hear them too.

'Margaret,' she said, in a strange voice, 'come here. Why have you left me? Do you know what they were saying, and what they expect me to believe?'

'Yes, I know,' returned Margaret, in her full

grave tone. 'I know how good God has been to you, and how grateful you will be for this mercy presently! Marjory,' putting her strong hands on her and lifting her to her feet as though she were a child, I think it will be better if you leave your mother to us for a little while. See how bewildered she is, and how feeble with her great trouble; and she is not able to speak to you.'

'Yes, leave us, Marjory,' acquiesced Mr. Frere, feeling how wise Margaret was in this; but Marjory still lingered. She cast a look of anguish at her mother; to their surprise, Mrs. Carr answered the look.

'Go, my child!' she said very gently; 'you shall come back to me as soon as I am able to bear it.'

She held out her hand to her, with a gesture that seemed to dismiss her; and poor Marjory turned away, feeling as though her heart were broken.

Mr. Frere followed her to the door.

'Do not fret,' he whispered; 'it will take time, and she is very ill. Go to Barry, my darling! your news will make him so happy.'

It was well that they had sent Marjory

away, for a most painful hour followed her dismissal. For a long time Mrs. Carr refused to believe their statement; Miriam's confession was read to her, but it seemed as though her passionate love for Lilias kept her incredulous.

Mr. Frere was very patient with her. He told her of Marjory's generosity and silence; how she had lived under her mother's roof as a guest, that she might teach them to love her; he reminded her of that evening in the wood, and how Marjory had told them her own story; and how she had made herself an exile, and had gone away for Lilias's sake.

'It was for Lilias!' he finished; and it was not until he had said this again and again that the stony incredulity vanished.

'She went away for Lilias!' she said, and her lips quivered; but before they could answer, she burst into bitter weeping. They understood her to say, between her sobs, that she blessed God that He had taken her darling, for she could not have lived, knowing this. Then they heard her say that she was a miserable inhuman mother, who did not know her own child; that Philip's child had all these years been an outcast and stranger. And then she put up her hands as though she were praying, her lips moved convulsively, and tears rolled down her cheeks. Was it for herself she was praying? they wondered; was she asking that the bitter wrong might be made right; and the power of loving this unknown child might be given to her? 'Lilias loved her—and it was for Lilias she did it,' they heard her murmur as she leant back in her chair, with closed eyelids and a spent exhausted look on her face.

'You may leave her to me,' Margaret whispered; 'my father will be here presently, and he will give her a composing draught. The worst is over now, but we must give her time to recover; the shock has been terrible.' And then she said in a still lower voice, 'Marjory must be patient; any more excitement would endanger the brain.'

'Poor child!' he sighed, as he went in search of her; 'it is a miserable business altogether. She will have need of patience for some time yet. Mrs. Carr is ill, very ill; she will be better left alone with Margaret.'

He found Marjory sitting by Barry's couch; their hands were tightly locked together. At Mr.

Frere's appearance the poor lad hailed him rapturously.

'Isn't it almost too good to be true?' he exclaimed, his eyes brilliant with joy. 'Now I know why she was always so good to me, and why I was so fond of her. It is not that I ever forget Lilias,' with a boyish sob; 'but it makes me less unhappy to know Marjory is my own sister, and that my mother will have some one to comfort her.'

'Barry, will you spare her to me a little while?' he said presently, when they had talked together a little. And when Barry had agreed to this reluctantly, he took her out into the fresh evening air, and told her all that had passed.

'Marjory,' he said, looking down into her sorrowful face with great tenderness; 'it was far better for you to go away as you did; you will have to be patient a little longer, for Miss Ainslie seems to fear the effect of any more excitement at present. We will stay here quietly, darling, and we will bide our time; and we will send for Anne to join us—that was a kind thought of Barry's. And you will be good and patient until the cloud lifts from your mother's brain, and she can realize all we have told her.' And Marjory promised, with many tears, that she would do her best.

It was a great comfort to them all when Anne arrived. Barry took a great fancy to her, and he allowed Marjory to leave him with tolerable grace when Miss Frere took her place. She told him those long walks and drives with Capel were indispensable to his sister just now; they quieted her, and assuaged her restlessness, when day after day passed, and she was not summoned to her mother's room, where Margaret alone kept watch and ward.

Margaret spoke very little of her patient to anyone. She lay very quiet, almost in a stupor, she told them; but she did not add that a strange expression crossed her face every time Marjory's footstep passed her door. Neither did she repeat to them the words that now and then escaped her lips.

'She thinks—she does nothing but think,' she said once to Mr. Frere. 'But for narcotics she would not sleep at all. There are streaks of grey in her hair—Marjory will be sorry for that.'

But one evening, when Marjory had retired

to her room for the night, there was a hasty knock at her door, and Margaret entered.

'Marjory,' she said, and there was a flush on her face; 'would you come with me a moment? Your mother is restless to-night; and I find there is something on her mind. She wants to see the mark on your arm that Mr. Frere described. Will you show it to her? You need not speak to her unless she speaks to you.'

Marjory was standing by the toilet-table brushing out her long brown hair. As Margaret spoke, the ivory brush dropped from her hand. Her mother had asked to see her at last.

'You must come just as you are,' went on Margaret, wondering a little over Marjory's beauty, as she stood there with her white dressing-gown falling to her feet, and her magnificent hair looking like a dusky veil in the dim light. 'I think'—very softly—'you will remind her now of the little child she lost eighteen years ago.'

Margaret hardly knew why she said this, except that there was something so pure and childlike in Marjory's appearance to-night.

Marjory did not answer, as she followed her

with a beating heart across the passage. As she entered the room her eyes turned involuntarily to the door that led into Lilias's room. It was closed for the first time; but the mother's face was turned to it, as she lay supported with pillows. She had lain thus day and night, but at the sound of Marjory's footstep she moved slightly, and a look of recognition came into her eyes.

Marjory bent over her. How white and sunken the face was, and yet there was a faint welcoming smile on the lips.

'You wished to see this, dear mother,' said Marjory gently, baring her white arm that the strange mark might be visible. Margaret was holding a candle behind her. Mrs. Carr raised herself with difficulty, and to Marjory's intense surprise she felt her mother's lips pressed against her arm.

'It is true,' she said, a little faintly. 'Marjory, will you forgive your mother for her long doubt?' She held out her arms as she spoke, and as Marjory nestled into them, she felt her mother's kisses on her hair and face.

'You may leave us, Margaret,' she said presently. 'My child will take care of me a little while.' And when they were left alone she motioned Marjory to take the seat beside her, and drew her face down on the pillow.

'I am so weak,' she sighed, 'but I like to feel you near me. I have wanted you all these days, Marjory; but I had no strength to send for you. Can you forgive me, my child, for my sin of ignorance all these years?'

'Mother,' she remonstrated, 'what is there to forgive? Let me love you and wait on you —that is all I ask now.' And then she whispered: 'Dear Lilias would be very happy to know that I am here to take care of you.'

A look of deep sadness crossed Mrs. Carr's face, and then she took her child's hands and held them to her breast.

'I have wronged you,' she said, in a low voice. 'I gave her all my mother's love. God knows I almost worshipped her. And now, what am I to do for you, my child?' speaking almost with the agony of the patriarch when Esau wept and pleaded for a blessing. The bitterness of this self-reproach touched Marjory's generous soul.

'Mother!' she said passionately, 'you are not to trouble about your want of love for me.

I know you are fond of me—you always have been; and I will not take Lilias's place. I am not jealous of your love for her. Dear mother, you shall love her as much as ever, and by-and-by you will love me too.' And as she said these noble words, she felt her mother's tears upon her face, and words that were almost a blessing came to her ears.

'God do so to me, and more also, if I do not love the child I brought into the world. Be patient, Marjory; be patient with your mother, and all will be right!'

CHAPTER XVII.

CONCLUSION.

MORE than two years had passed since Lilias's death. It was Christmas Eve, and a family party were gathered in Cosy Nook.

A mighty fagot blazed upon the hearth, and the ruddy gleams lighted up the old hall and threw crimson reflections through the bay-window upon the snow.

The carol-singers had been up to Mavisbank, and they could hear the boys' voices still dying away in the distance. Mrs. Carr was listening to them as she sat in her high-backed chair.

These two years had left their traces upon her. There were silver threads now in the dark hair, and lines on the smooth forehead;

but the sweet tranquillity of her expression spoke of strength gained by submission and a chastened will. In repose, there was still a look of sadness; but it passed away when she spoke.

Anne sat knitting beside her—still the same blithe busy little soul. Barry still occupied his couch, but his crutches were always near him, ready for use; and he was no longer idle and suffering. Life meant work to him as well as to others, and was making him manly and self-reliant.

Mr. Frere was in his favourite attitude on the rug, declaiming to his women-folk; but every now and then he broke off a sentence restlessly, as though listening for some footsteps that he missed. As the door opened a subtle change passed over his face, for there was his wife crossing the hall in her velvet gown, and in her arms she held his boy; and though he made no movement to meet her, his eyes brightened at the sight.

'Look, mother dear!' cried Marjory, in her joyous young voice; 'the carol-singers woke the boy, and now nothing will do but he must come down to his grandmother;' and she placed the rosy laughing fellow in the arms that were always ready to receive him.

'What does Aunt Anne say to such infringement of nursery discipline?' observed Mrs. Carr, with a loving glance at her daughter.

'Anne says,' returned that individual quietly, 'that his grandmother will spoil him as much as she spoils his mother.'

'Do I spoil you, Marjory?' asked Mrs. Carr, with a happy smile; but there was no need for Marjory to answer, only that long tender look between them spoke of a perfect understanding between mother and daughter.

'Marjory,' observed Mr. Frere, in his whimsical way, 'I begin to feel neglected; and, in point of fact, so does Barry. There is a preponderance of females at the present moment that makes the other sex uneasy.'

'Not if we include baby,' interrupted Marjory audaciously, but she slid her hand in her husband's arm as she spoke.

'He is under age, and I decline to give him a vote,' returned Mr. Frere scornfully. 'A creature who can only enunciate a single letter of the alphabet, and is for ever gurgling "Ah, ah!" over his rattle—and of all things I hate rattles—can hardly be pronounced a reasonable human creature; perhaps, being his father's son, he may in time develop an inherited precocity of intellect.'

'Poor little darling, I am sure of that!' returned the young mother proudly.

'My dear,' replied Mr. Frere sententiously, 'with such parents, such a hope is well authorized; but, as usual, you have interrupted me, Marjory. I had taken up my parable on the subject of mothers-in-law.

'The nineteenth century is a reforming age. We are reforming prisons, lunatic asylums, workhouses, and the dwellings of the poor. Perhaps there is a little too much dynamite, but I hope we may put a stop to that. Well, there is still an abuse that I should like to reform. I consider that mothers-in-law have been hardly used; they are much spoken against in private life. *Punch* has caricatured them mercilessly. They have become a byword and a terror, so that many a young man of feeble organization has eschewed matrimony except with a motherless orphan. As motherless orphans are not plentiful, except in workhouses, the world, in time, will be depopulated.

'Now I wish to write an article on behalf of this much-abused class of women. As a man and a husband, I feel my sensibilities awakened on this point. Good heavens! may not my son one day cease to gurgle everlasting "Ah, ah's!" and take to himself a wife? and then, Marjory, you will be a mother-in-law yourself.'

Marjory clapped her hands.

'Is it not good to hear him, Anne?' she said, with her old merry laugh.

'My dear'—with a furtively admiring glance at her happy face—'you have broken the flow of my eloquence. I was going to point out—not that it matters—that we ourselves were ready to testify to the excellence of mothers-in-law. I consider myself fortunate in my own case. Thanks to your mother, Marjory, we have two homes; when we are tired of Murrel's End, we decamp with the baby, his rattles, Anne, and the devoted Mackay, and take up our abode at Mavisbank. No one gives us notice to quit; no one hints that our absence would be desirable. When we hold up our finger, your mother appears at Murrel's End; and she is so pleasant—she falls in so entirely with my habits—that I forget she is not my own mother;'

in fact, I wish she were—at least—— Come, now, my meaning is involved, and Barry is squaring his fists at me.'

'Hush, love!' whispered Marjory; 'I think I hear footsteps—that must be Hurrell.'

Yes; when they opened the door, it was Hurrell, and Lassie was with him. He came among them looking a little graver, a little older, and a little browner; for since Mrs. Wentworth's death—eighteen months ago—he had travelled much.

'Mother,' he said, as he sat down by Mrs. Carr—for he had called her by this name for a long time—'I have done what you wished; and you were right, as you always are—Margaret has promised to be my wife.'

'Dear Hurrell!' she replied, lifting up her face to kiss him; but though there were tears in her eyes, there was no sadness at all in her voice. 'You have made me very happy. Margaret has loved you all her life; and, but for seeing my child'—here she faltered a little—'you would have married her long ago.'

'Yes,' he said gravely; 'I know that now.'

'Hush!' broke in Marjory's clear voice; 'there are the carol-singers coming back from the Vicarage. Let us go to the door, Capel;' and she drew him gently to the threshold.

'Nowel, Nowel!' sang the children's voices; outside, the moonbeams shone on the crisp, hard snow.

Anne, who had followed them, felt her hand taken; with the other, Marjory was clinging to her husband's arm.

'Do you remember,' she said, in a low voice, 'the little child that came to you both out from the snow?'

'God bless the day that brought us that little child!' returned Mr. Frere fervently, in a still lower tone.

But Anne heard it, and said:

'Amen!'

THE END.

BILLING AND SONS, PRINTERS, GUILDFORD.
G., C. & Co.

www.ingramcontent.com/pod-product-compliance
Lightning Source LLC
Chambersburg PA
CBHW022028240426
43667CB00042B/1283